# MY FATHER AND ALBERT EINSTEIN

# MY FATHER AND ALBERT EINSTEIN

◆

Biography of a Department Store owner, whose thirst for knowledge enabled his close friendship with a genius who changed man's concepts of the universe

*Joan Rothman Brill*

iUniverse, Inc.
New York  Lincoln  Shanghai

# MY FATHER AND ALBERT EINSTEIN

**Biography of a Department Store owner, whose thirst for knowledge enabled his close friendship with a genius who changed man's concepts of the universe**

Copyright © 2008 by Joan R. Brill

All rights reserved. No part of this book may be used or reproduced by any means, graphic, electronic, or mechanical, including photocopying, recording, taping or by any information storage retrieval system without the written permission of the publisher except in the case of brief quotations embodied in critical articles and reviews.

iUniverse books may be ordered through booksellers or by contacting:

iUniverse
2021 Pine Lake Road, Suite 100
Lincoln, NE 68512
www.iuniverse.com
1-800-Authors (1-800-288-4677)

Because of the dynamic nature of the Internet, any Web addresses or links contained in this book may have changed since publication and may no longer be valid.

The views expressed in this work are solely those of the author and do not necessarily reflect the views of the publisher, and the publisher hereby disclaims any responsibility for them.

David Rothman's tape recordings are copyrighted and registered in the Library of Congress, 1963.

ISBN: 978-0-595-47416-5 (pbk)
ISBN: 978-0-595-91694-8 (ebk)

Printed in the United States of America

*I would like to dedicate this book to my daughter,
Leslie Lynn Brill Davidson b. September 26, 1953.*

*Leslie spent much of her time promoting this project before her untimely death on November 4, 2005. I like to think that she would have approved of my completion of this book. Here she is with her husband, Dr. Arthur Davidson.*

*I would also like to dedicate this book to my father,
David Arthur Rothman, b. September 14, 1896 d.November 19, 1981*

*Without his taped narration, we would not have this complete record of his unusual and beautiful friendship with Dr. Albert Einstein.*

# Contents

List of Illustrations . . . . . . . . . . . . . . . . . . . . . . . . . . . . . . . . ix
Introduction . . . . . . . . . . . . . . . . . . . . . . . . . . . . . . . . . . . . . xi

## ALBERT EINSTEIN—As I knew Him

| CHAPTER 1 | The Beginning of a Friendship . . . . . . . . . . . . . . . . . . 3 |
| CHAPTER 2 | Music and Musing. . . . . . . . . . . . . . . . . . . . . . . . . . . 8 |
| CHAPTER 3 | An Evening of Chamber Music . . . . . . . . . . . . . . . . 13 |
| CHAPTER 4 | A Near Tragedy. . . . . . . . . . . . . . . . . . . . . . . . . . . . . 16 |
| CHAPTER 5 | Various Anecdotes. . . . . . . . . . . . . . . . . . . . . . . . . . . 18 |
| CHAPTER 6 | Bigraphical Background of David Arthur Rothman. . . . . . . . . . . . . . . . . . . . . . . . . . . . . . . . . . . 22 |
| CHAPTER 7 | My Mother Ruth Samuel Rothman. . . . . . . . . . . . . 37 |
| CHAPTER 8 | A Diary of Love and Marriage . . . . . . . . . . . . . . . . . 45 |
| CHAPTER 9 | Armistice Day . . . . . . . . . . . . . . . . . . . . . . . . . . . . . 68 |
| CHAPTER 10 | The Flu Epidemic of 1918. . . . . . . . . . . . . . . . . . . . 79 |
| CHAPTER 11 | Some Signs of the Times . . . . . . . . . . . . . . . . . . . . . 87 |
| CHAPTER 12 | Beliefs and Miscellany . . . . . . . . . . . . . . . . . . . . . . . 89 |
| CHAPTER 13 | An Unforgettable Evening of Chamber Music. . . . . . 92 |
| CHAPTER 14 | Dealing with Crowds. . . . . . . . . . . . . . . . . . . . . . . . 96 |
| CHAPTER 15 | Another historic close call . . . . . . . . . . . . . . . . . . . 100 |

| | | |
|---|---|---|
| CHAPTER 16 | Our Walks Together | 102 |
| CHAPTER 17 | A Lesson in Relativity | 110 |
| CHAPTER 18 | A Fond Farewell | 117 |
| CHAPTER 19 | Letters | 119 |
| CHAPTER 20 | A Visit to Albert Einstein in Princeton | 124 |
| CHAPTER 21 | The End of the Story | 126 |
| APPENDIX A | The Einstein Miracles by Dr. Jerold M. Lowenstein | 131 |
| APPENDIX B | The Einstein Family | 137 |
| APPENDIX C | The Rothman-Samuel family | 139 |
| Acknowledgements | | 143 |
| About the Author | | 145 |

# List of Illustrations

David Rothman in Rothman's Department Store c. 1936 . . . . . . . . . . . . . . . . . . . 4
The Rothman Sundial. . . . . . . . . . . . . . . . . . . . . . . . . . . . . . . . . . . . . . . . . . . . . . 6
Chaim (Charles) Rothman. . . . . . . . . . . . . . . . . . . . . . . . . . . . . . . . . . . . . . . .23
Apothecary Bottles . . . . . . . . . . . . . . . . . . . . . . . . . . . . . . . . . . . . . . . . . . . . . .25
Letter to Joan Rothman from Benjamin Britten . . . . . . . . . . . . . . . . . . . . . . .31
David Rothman and Benjamin Britten . . . . . . . . . . . . . . . . . . . . . . . . . . . . . .33
Dad's telescope. . . . . . . . . . . . . . . . . . . . . . . . . . . . . . . . . . . . . . . . . . . . . . . . .34
Nana's Vase . . . . . . . . . . . . . . . . . . . . . . . . . . . . . . . . . . . . . . . . . . . . . . . . . . .39
Necklace and opera glasses . . . . . . . . . . . . . . . . . . . . . . . . . . . . . . . . . . . . . . .40
Braided Rug . . . . . . . . . . . . . . . . . . . . . . . . . . . . . . . . . . . . . . . . . . . . . . . . . . .41
Suffolk Friend of Music Orchestra flyer- Benjamin Britten . . . . . . . . . . . . . . .43
First page of Diary. . . . . . . . . . . . . . . . . . . . . . . . . . . . . . . . . . . . . . . . . . . . . .46
The Samuel Family. . . . . . . . . . . . . . . . . . . . . . . . . . . . . . . . . . . . . . . . . . . . .48
"Nana"—Aunt Regina Noé Sturmdorf. . . . . . . . . . . . . . . . . . . . . . . . . . . . . .49
Ruth Rothman playing her new piano. . . . . . . . . . . . . . . . . . . . . . . . . . . . . . .65
MS Pilsudski poster . . . . . . . . . . . . . . . . . . . . . . . . . . . . . . . . . . . . . . . . . . . . .88
Einstein and Dr. Valentine Bargmann . . . . . . . . . . . . . . . . . . . . . . . . . . . . . . .95
Walking . . . . . . . . . . . . . . . . . . . . . . . . . . . . . . . . . . . . . . . . . . . . . . . . . . . . .103
Dad and Einstein sitting on a rock . . . . . . . . . . . . . . . . . . . . . . . . . . . . . . . .105

*More Walking* .................................................. *106*

*Albert Einstein in Nassau Point, Long Island, New York* ................. *107*

*Theory of Relativity in brief* ....................................... *108*

*Joseph Scharl poster—Hofstra Centennial Celebration* .................. *112*

*Joseph Scharl painting* ........................................... *114*

*Letter* ........................................................ *120*

*Ruth and David Rothman's 60$^{th}$ Anniversary* ......................... *128*

*Einstein and Dad sitting on a boat gunwale* .......................... *129*

*Rothman's Department Store—2007* ................................ *130*

*Bob and Ronnie Rothman* ........................................ *130*

# *Introduction*

This is really a book about my father, David Arthur Rothman (1896–1981.)

In 1963, I was pursuing a BA Degree from Southampton College of Long Island University. A term paper was required for my biology class, but I told Dr. Jay Barton that I would truly like to write a paper about my father's friendship with Dr. Albert Einstein. Permission was granted; so I asked my Dad to record all of his recollections about the friendship.

It seems that Dad had total recall of all that had occurred during the friendship, and he took great joy in sharing these stories with all who were interested. And it seems that *everyone* loved hearing the stories.

Dad recorded all of his memories on reel-to-reel tape, over a period of about two months. Then I transcribed Dad's narrative for the term paper. Dad was interviewed many times by many writers, local and national. Usually, he was annoyed when he learned how his words were changed and distorted. Therefore, I have decided to present Dad's recollections in his own words as much as possible. I will add my own comments in italics, and try to provide the background that Dad omitted, because he knew that I knew it.

Later in this story, I will add details from Dad's early life, stories from his marriage in 1918, and the diary that Mom and Dad wrote during their early relationship. I'm sure that they would have been proud to have it published, because they always said that we would find it some day after they were both gone. My husband, Paul Kallmeyer, did find it, up on a shelf in a closet, in the house that they shared for over 62 years.

What was the chain of events that brought the Albert Einstein family to Southold, New York in the summer of 1939? Einstein was born on March 14, 1879, in Ulm, Germany. His parents were Pauline and Hermann Einstein.

Einstein studied the violin from the age of six until he was thirteen, and gained a love for that instrument and music that lasted throughout his life. In 1895, he finished high school in Aarau, Switzerland and then enrolled at the Swiss Federal Polytechnic School in Zurich, graduating in 1900 with a degree in physics. After graduation, he could not find a university position, so he took a job working for the patent office in Bern, Switzerland. This gave him a great deal of time to contemplate scientific theories.

In 1914, Einstein went to Berlin, and later became head of the Kaiser Wilhelm Physical Institute, where he was a Special Professor, at the University of Berlin.

In 1933, when Einstein and his family were threatened by the rise of Nazism and Hitler, they left Germany. Eventually the family settled in the United States, and Einstein accepted a position at the Institute for Advanced Study in Princeton, New Jersey.

From Dad's narration, it seems that Einstein and his entire family had taken a trip to California, probably to see Einstein's son, Dr. Hans Albert Einstein, b. 1904, who was a Professor of Hydraulic Engineering in California. Then the entire family, including Hans Albert, traveled cross-country to Southold for a summer vacation. The household included Einstein, Einstein's son who was apparently nicknamed Harry, Harry's wife Frieda and their son Hadi, Einstein's step-daughter Margot, Einstein's sister Maja, and the secretary, Miss Helen Dukas. For more details, see Appendix B.

# ALBERT EINSTEIN—As
I knew Him

# 1

# *The Beginning of a Friendship*

*This is my Dad speaking, as he recorded on reel-to-reel tape over a period of about two months, in 1963:*

And so, Joan, as you wanted me to, I'm about to relate the story of my friendship with Albert Einstein during the summer of 1939.

Probably the first thing that you would want to know is how it came about that we met—how it all started, that summer of 1939 in Southold. Well, the rumor had been going about town that Albert Einstein was to come to Southold for the summer. When I heard this, I was deeply interested, and somewhat excited, because it had always been a dream of mine that some day I might be able to meet him.

*I must explain here that my father had a hardware store, Rothman's Department Store, in the small town of Southold, on the North Fork of Long Island, NY. The store was founded in 1919 when my family moved to Southold from Bayonne, New Jersey. Dad sold GE Appliances, clothing, cameras and whatever items were in demand. The store was connected to the house where we lived, and that made it very convenient for all. There was a bell that rang when a customer opened the door, so that Dad was able to spend much time in the house, until he was needed in the store. The store is still there in Southold in 2007, and is being run by my brother Bob Rothman and his son Ronnie.*

*Here's an early (c.1935) photo of Rothman's Department Store. That's David Rothman waiting for a customer to arrive:*

*Dad continues:* I had almost forgotten about Einstein's arrival in Southold when one day in walked a young lady, and of course I immediately recognized her as being Einstein's step-daughter, Margot *(Einstein Lowenthal.)* I didn't let on, but went over to her and asked her what I could do for her. She described the need for a sharpening stone which was used for sculpturing instruments. As she described it, I realized that I had this item. It had been lying around the store for years. I had acquired it from another store that had gone out of business some years before. It was among some odds and ends that they had left, after the closing-out sale.

When I dug it out and showed it to her, she said that it was just what she was looking for. It had a mark of $6.00 across it in crayon. I could see that she noticed the price on it, and that her face fell a little bit. She said to me, "You know, I have searched for this all the way from California to Southold; and now that I have found it, I see that I cannot afford it!"

I replied, "Look, I should like to present this to you as a little gift."

"Oh, no, I could not take this," she said.

"But there is a condition," I answered.

"And what would that be?" she asked.

I said, "Only that every time you use it, you must think of me."

She insisted that she wouldn't take it, but I assured her that I had no use for the sharpening stone, and would probably never sell it. I finally persuaded her to accept it. She seemed a little embarrassed, but I made her feel at ease as best I could. As I was putting it in a bag to give it to her, I said, "And how is your illustrious father these days?"

She looked at me with great surprise and said, "Do you know me?"

I said, "Of course. I have always followed the doings of your father and family in the newspaper articles and magazines, so I would know you anywhere." She told me that her father was very well, and that they had had a long trip from California to Southold. After some small conversation, she left.

During the following morning, I had the Mozart G minor Symphony No. 40 playing on the phonograph in the store when the door opened, and in he walked! Behind him, his sister, Maja *(Einstein Winterler)* was followed by Einstein's son, Dr. Harry Einstein, Harry's wife Frieda, and the grandson, Hadi.

Well, I walked over to turn the phonograph down a little; but Einstein said, "Please do not touch it. Leave it. Let it play—it is bea-u-ti-ful!"

He started to wave his arms up in the air, humming and singing, and beating time to the music as if he were conducting it. He seemed to be enjoying it immensely, so I let it play until it finished.

*We are so used to hearing classical music today, on National Public Radio stations and recordings, that we take it for granted. However, in 1939, classical music was much less accessible! In Southold, most of my school friends were unfamiliar with classical music. I was only nine in 1939, but I was already studying the piano and playing some rather difficult classical music including Chopin's Fantasie-Impromptu, Op. 66. My school friends laughed at me for my taste in music!*

*However, my Dad used to clip coupons from the New York Post. When he had enough coupons, he would mail them in and would receive a recording (78 R.P.M.) of a major symphony ... Mozart, Hayden, Beethoven, Schubert, Tschaikovsky, etc.*

*In fact, when I attended the Juilliard School during 1948–1950, I was the only person in our Literature class who could identify all the symphonies after the first few notes, even though I was studying the* piano! *My teachers were quite surprised.*

Then Dr. Einstein came over to me and said, "My daughter has told me that this is a store where one can buy anything in the whole world, and" (looking about the place,) "now that I have seen it, I believe it."

*You must imagine the following dialogue recited with a strong German accent. Dad always related the stories complete with the accent. I wish that I could put it down on paper!*

I laughed a little, and he said, "Haff you any sundahls?" His accent was very heavy ... sometimes almost difficult to understand. You'd have to listen very carefully to get every word.

I wondered what in the world he would want a sundial for—perhaps for a scientific experiment—and I had none to sell. However, I owned one that was outside in the yard by the telescope, on the decorative pedestal that we have out there.

I said, "Maybe I can help you. If you will follow me, I will show you."

So he followed behind me looking rather puzzled, and the son Harry came with him. We went through the back door, out into the yard, and I showed him the sundial on the pedestal and said, "Now, if you can use this, you can take it and return it whenever you want to."

Well, he let out a belly-laugh, "Ho, Ho, Ho, Ho!" and he laughed and laughed. Finally he picked up his foot and showed me, "Sundahls."

I realized then that he meant *sandals*! I felt so could stupid and so embarrassed. I was hoping that the earth would part so that I could disappear into a hole in the ground! I guess he noticed it, for he said, "Do not feel badly. My English is so terrible. It is only mine atrocious accent!"

We all laughed and came back into the store. I took him up to the front, where I had a few pairs of sandals, and showed him what I had.

"Ach!" he said, "This is what I have been looking for all the way from California to Southold. I am very happy to have found them, and I would like to buy these."

They were $1.35. I wrapped them up and said, "It is evident that you love music also, among your other accomplishments."

"Oh, yes," he said.

"And do you play an instrument?" I asked.

He replied, "Yes, I play on the fiddle, but I am only an amateur."

I said, "Well, so am I. I play the fiddle, and I also am an amateur."

Einstein said, "Well, some day we must play together."

This was an indication of how friendly he could be. He hardly knew me, and yet he suggested that some day we should make music together.

So I said, "This I would like; but of course, the invitation must come from you, and you must name the time. I will be very happy to come if you really want me to." We made some small conversation about the location. Then, just as he was leaving he said, "You come Monday night?"

"It will be my pleasure," I replied.

Einstein said, "I have my violin, but not music."

I said, "Well, I have all kinds of music, and I will bring the music."

And so they all left, and you can imagine how I felt. I was simply flabbergasted. I was tingling all over with excitement. Here was a dream, a fabulous, impossible dream coming to pass—becoming a fact—becoming true. I walked on air all day.

# 2
## *Music and Musing*

As time went on, Monday night rolled around. I started to go through the music, and I just couldn't make up my mind what to bring. I didn't know how good a player he was, so I thought I'd take the Pleyel duets and, a little bit harder, maybe the Mazas duets. Then, if he were a *really* good player, I thought I'd have the Bach *Double Concerto* along—just in case.

I went down there and put the music down on the table. He already had his violin out, and was doing a few scales. He walked over to the table, looked at the music and saw the Pleyel duets.

He said, "Ach, this is trivial!"

He picked up the Mazas duets and said, "This is also trivial."

Then he spied the Bach "*Double*." "Ah! This is better!"

He started to play without looking at the music, and was walking around the room as he played, hitting every note with precision. I realized then that this man was a really fine violinist.

*I think that Dad, who was strictly amateur, was unduly impressed with Einstein's playing. Einstein was usually considered a fairly good amateur, but not terrific by professional standards. But apparently he was much better than my Dad, and that made a great impression!*

Thus, we sat down. He decided to play the first part, and I would do the second part. We started, and played about three measures when I fumbled and stopped. He didn't say anything, and we started again. This time, I played about sixteen measures, when again I slipped up.

I said, "Ah, first—I'm a little out of practice; and second—I feel nervous in your presence. I don't know why, but I have this feeling that I am playing with a really great man, and I feel nervous."

He laughed, "Ach," he said, "Let us try again." So we started again. I got about half way through, playing with a terrible tremolo, with a nervous grip on the bow. I played just terribly.

I said, "It's no use. We have to stop. I cannot do it."

Well, he was very understanding. He put his violin down, I put mine down; and with that, he invited me to come sit on the porch and visit with him a little.

It was a beautiful, warm evening. The moon was shining brightly, and it was just delightful sitting out there. At first we made some small talk. Then, finally, I brought the conversation around to conditions in Germany. I said to him, "You know, I am puzzled and amazed at how it was possible for a man like Hitler ... a nincompoop ... a megalomaniac ... an idiot ... a bigot ... to achieve the leadership of a nation as cultured as Germany."

He answered, "Ah, but you are wrong. Germany is not such a cultured nation. It is true that she may have a cultured minority, but the masses are very slow-thinking and somewhat dull-witted. They have always required someone to guide them—to lead them. Along with this trait, they have always had a tremendous ego. They are a very egotistical people, and unless this is corrected, some day it will destroy them. You will see. And as to how Hitler came to acquire the leadership in Germany—at first we all thought it was a huge joke and we all laughed at him; until one day we discovered that when we laughed, we had our faces slapped. By that time, we found it was too late to do anything about it."

Now, Joan, this statement was made in 1939, before Hitler had attacked Poland, before war had broken out in the United States. I thought you might want to know this.

Then, at one time, he asked me what I thought about the possibility of anti-Semitism breaking out in the United States the same way it had in Germany. I told him I thought that anything was possible; but that this was something that was highly improbable. I told him that many times I had seen such movements develop among the lunatic fringe, such as the Ku Klux Klan or the Bund, all of which were generally ridiculed and laughed out of existence. The only way I could see such a thing happening in this country was in the case of great economic distress, but this seemed improbable in the immediate future. However, I don't think he was very convinced. He was always a little bit suspicious about that point.

Then the conversation turned to great books. I told him something about myself; how at the age of thirteen I had just graduated public school, and that this had been all the education that was possible for me. I also mentioned how I had gone to work on the railroad as a telegrapher. Since I had a tremendous urge and curiosity to understand the nature of the universe and my relationship to it, I had set up for myself a plan of systematic study from which I had hoped to learn the general principles of the entire field of human knowledge. I had felt that there was no time for detail in the different subjects; so the first thing I had done was to prepare myself by studying logic and the scientific method. I first had read Kant and others on the beginning of things ... of nebula hypothesis, cosmology, inorganic evolution, down to the arrival of man; then anthropology, psychology, comparative religion, economics, history, physics, biology—in fact, every subject that would help me understand the nature of things. I studied Immanuel Kant, Herbert Spencer, Charles Darwin, Aldous Huxley, George Berkeley, Adam Smith, Ernst Haeckel, Sir James Jeans, and many others. I spent eight years in this pursuit while working nights on the railroad as a telegrapher.

*I remember Dad's experience while studying on the job when he was a station master for the Jersey Central Railroad. He was busy reading when a gentleman interrupted him and scolded him for not paying attention to work. Dad was not too polite, but then he learned that he was speaking to one of the high official of the Jersey Central. Dad was about to be fired; but when the official saw what Dad was reading, and how hard he was studying, he forgave Dad! So Dad kept his job on the railroad, until he decided to take his family to Southold, Long Island. But more about that later.*

When I was about eighteen, I thought that I could recreate the entire universe, given a little of the primordial matter ... that is, until Einstein came along. Then my universe collapsed. Matter, energy, time, space, the aluminiferous ether, light, gravitation, motion, inertia ... all these concepts I had to change. Nothing was right, so I gave up. I figured that this was too much for me ... especially without a knowledge of mathematics.

Mathematics was the one subject that I failed to master. Without early training and a good teacher, I found math a subject that was impossible for me.

Dr. Einstein laughed and said, "Well, some day soon we must straighten all this out."

What amazed me was that the very same thinkers that I admired so much, and spent so much time studying, were the same ones that he admired in his youth. He was a great lover of Haeckel and Herbert Spencer, and Huxley. They were his favorites.

I went on to tell him how the one thing that cropped up in my mind most often was why a rod contracted in the direction of its motion, and why a clock could change its rhythm in the same way. I could make neither head nor tail of this riddle.

Dr. Einstein said, "This we must straighten out."

I told him that I had no knowledge of mathematics, and that I understood this to be a very difficult concept without such knowledge. He said that this was not so.

"On the other hand," he said, "If one cannot explain this subject without recourse to mathematics—if he cannot do this in simple language—then he does not know his subject well."

Thus we talked for quite a while. Then he said, "With regard to the contraction of a rod in the direction of its motion ... if one has some understanding of molecular activity, it is possible to explain it; and this we shall do sometime."

Joan, I must tell you something very interesting about his love life. You know, at the time when I first met him, Mom was having a nervous breakdown and was away receiving treatment. That first evening when we were together on the porch, I told him about my trouble, and how I was suffering so much because of it ... how I loved Mom so deeply that this came to me as a terrible tragedy. I was just about beside myself all of the time, running back and forth to the hospital every other day. I told him about ourselves a little bit, stressing somewhat how we loved each other.

He said to me, "You know, I have had two wives, and I have never experienced a love of that kind. I must say that with me, it was a matter of respect for my wives, and a feeling of gratefulness for the care that they gave me. As for the type of love that you describe, this I have never experienced."

His involvement with work left him little time for other interests.

Well, I can't remember all the details of the conversation on that particular evening, but suddenly Miss Dukas, his secretary, appeared.

"Mr. Rothman, you are keeping the Doctor up so late! It is almost midnight. I think it is time to stop."

Professor Einstein said, "On the other hand, *I* am keeping *Mr. Rothman* up!"

At any rate, I said to him, "As a musical evening, it was a grand failure; but as for our conversation, I enjoyed this very much. And to make up for the musical aspects of the evening, next week I shall bring some friends, and we can have a string quartet."

"This would please me very much," he replied.

By this time, the son Harry had appeared on the scene. I was saying "Good Night" to him, and as I walked to the door, Harry followed me and said, in an aside, **"But Mr. Rothman, these must not be jazz musicians!"**

I said, "Oh no! Nothing like that. We will play Hayden and Mozart and Beethoven Quartets, and I'm sure it will be very nice. Do not worry."

And I left.

The impressions I had of Einstein that evening were that of a very sincere, kindly, shy, gentle, sweet-natured, intensely human, very modest, considerate, truly marvelous character. He was almost "Christ-like"—not in the sense that he was a God, but in the sense that his was the character of a Christ. I detected a strong sense of social justice, a great sense of humor, very little regard for conventional things. He wore a plain pair of duck pants with a rope around his waist for a belt—but he was very clean—immaculate. I remember him best as he waved the flies away from the dinner table. He refused to kill them, or even to fish. To him, all living creatures were sacred; and he was the paragon of gentleness.

Of course, I came away quite excited, with a sense of exhilaration, at the realization of having sat and talked with this great and famous man throughout the entire evening. I was thrilled that he was willing to sit there until midnight talking to me, and—I don't know how to say it—but I just felt that he was enjoying it! It was a source of great amazement to me. I have always had that feeling of wonderment that this thing had come about.

# 3

## *An Evening of Chamber Music*

After my failed "violin duet" evening with Dr. Einstein, I thought I'd better arrange for the string quartet. I called your Uncle Milton Samuel. (*Milton was my mother's brother, and he was a professional violinist. He had studied in Paris, and Sarah Bernhardt had given him a violin bow with a mother-of-pearl handle because she liked him so much. Milton's grandmother, Johanna Noé, was a seamstress for the great actress.*)

Well, I had a hard time convincing Milton and the other players that Albert Einstein was going to be one of the players! They just wouldn't believe it; but they all agreed to meet. I heard the violinist's wife, Florrie, while I was talking to him on the telephone, say, "Who's that calling?"

He replied, "Oh, it's that Dave Rothman. As usual, he's kibitzing around. He says he wants me to play string quartets with Albert Einstein! But you know Dave...."

And that's the way it was. None of them believed it.

At any rate, they met at my home, as indicated, the idea being that I wanted to brief them on how to act before we moved to the Einstein residence. I wanted to be sure that when they got there they would behave in a natural manner, without "kow-towing," and would treat him just like anybody else who was there to play string quartets. I knew this was important, if it were to be successful. Thus, we all met; they came, and I briefed them, and we all drove to Einstein's house. They *still* thought I was up to some joke until they walked into the living room and spotted him.

When we came in, Milton brought a table he had made ... a combination music stand and table. When we brought it in and set it up, Einstein said, "My, My! Real Capitalistic!" He thought that was quite a luxury.

The entire Einstein family was there, and I supposed I should tell you a little bit about the place. There weren't enough chairs—but there were three orange crates, and we used them for chairs, believe it or not. I sat on one, Margot on another, and Miss Dukas, the secretary, sat on another. Mrs. Winterler had a chair, as did Harry Einstein and his wife. Thus the evening started.

They played some Hayden first. I was permitted to sit in on the slow movement, and it really sounded beautiful. It was then that I discovered just how good a violinist Albert Einstein really was. He played with preciseness and with feeling. His face just shone as he made the music.

It seems that the 'cellist played with a rather weak sound. There wasn't too much power to her playing; and at the end of the first portion, just before the intermission, Einstein said to her, "Young lady, you must ZOOM oudt!" I thought that quite funny ... the way he put it.

It was a wonderful evening of music. We stopped for coffee and doughnuts, and we talked a little bit. Everybody behaved naturally. When we left, I could see that everybody had had a good time. Miss Dukas and Margot told me how beautiful it was, and hoped that we could do it again. I was very happy about the whole thing.

By the way, when I had mentioned bringing quartet players at first, Einstein had said, "I hope that they are not professional. You know, I find them entirely too critical."

I understood what he meant, and I reassured him on that point.

During subsequent sessions, we were able to get a man named Eamons, a 'cellist with the Philharmonic, and we pawned him off as an amateur. We warned him that one slip, and we were sunk. This we were able to carry off right through. He never gave any indication of being professional. You can imagine how beautiful the music sounded with a fellow like that playing the 'cello! Simply marvelous!

Joan, you probably heard some of those quartets when you were very young.

*Yes, some of the sessions were at the Rothman home, and I was there to listen to the music, and meet the musicians. I was only nine, but I do remember the excitement.*

However, this Eamons gave me a little annoyance. One evening during one of the intermissions, he said to Einstein, "What do you say, Professor? I have a couple of tickets to the Princeton-Yale football game. What do you say ... would you like to come along with me and take in the game?"

I saw Einstein's eyes open up in surprise, and he said, "NO! I do not like to see people jumping up and down like so many monkeys!"

Boy, that pleased me, because I was a little annoyed. It was the kind of thing I tried to avoid.

Another time Eamons pulled out a batch of personal cards with his name on them, and handed them to Einstein during intermission and asked Einstein to autograph them. Well, Einstein did it … and seemed to think nothing of it. But it certainly annoyed me! I was hoping this wouldn't happen.

*The chamber music sessions became a highlight of that summer of 1939, for Einstein, for Dad, and for all of the players. Einstein never failed to refer to those wonderful evenings in his letters and in all of his communications with my Dad. I'm sure that the evenings were also memorable for those who stood on the porch outside and peered in the windows!*

# 4

## *A Near Tragedy*

And now, Joan, I'd like to tell you about an incident that very few people know anything about. It's funny that it missed the newspapers. Nothing was ever written about it ... It seems that no one ever heard about it at all.

One morning, Einstein and his sister, Mrs. Winterler, decided to go sailing. Einstein was in the bow of the boat raising the sail. It was hoisted just about all the way when a gust of wind capsized the boat. Both of them went into the drink, and neither of them could swim a stroke. Somehow they managed to grab the boat and hang on. There they were, and if it hadn't been for a fifteen-year-old boy who lived opposite them and spotted them, I don't know what would have happened.

This young boy spotted them, ran down to the beach, swam out, and pulled in the boat, with Dr. Einstein and Mrs. Winterler hanging on to it.

When I heard about this, I went down to make sure everything was all right. When I asked what had happened, Einstein said, "Well you know, I made a triple error ... There are three possible errors:

1. I could have hoisted the sail before I pulled up the anchor. 2. I could have hoisted the anchor before I pulled up the sail. 3. I should have had life preservers with me."

Einstein thought it was a big joke, but I didn't. You know, this happened before he had written that famous letter to President Franklin Delano Roosevelt suggesting the possibility of making an atomic bomb before the Germans did. I wonder what the course of history would have been had he lost his life at that particular time. How close the course of future events came to being changed!

It was shortly after this incident that he did write that famous letter to President Roosevelt; and while I was with him incessantly at that time, he never breathed a word of it to me. He never said anything about it, although we discussed atomistic physics quite a bit while he was trying to explain the different concepts. There was not one word about that matter at all.

*All of this took place during the summer of 1939. On August 2, 1939, scientist Leo Szilard visited Einstein in Nassau Point, Peconic, Long Island, to request that Einstein write the now-famous letter to President Roosevelt. Einstein explained that it was now possible to manufacture an atomic bomb; and that Germany was already attempting to do so. This bomb was possible only because of the scientific theories that Einstein had developed.*

*The rest is history. After the United States dropped atomic bombs on Hiroshima and Nagasaki, and killed so many people, Einstein held himself personally responsible, and often discussed his feelings of guilt and sadness at what had occurred. His theories ($e=mc^2$) had made this monster bomb possible!*

*By the way, Dad referred to Einstein as Dr. Einstein. Dad once told me that he questioned Einstein about how he preferred to be addressed. Einstein replied that he had* earned *the doctorate. It was an earned title, rather than one bestowed upon him; and therefore he preferred to be called "Dr. Einstein."*

*It seems that many people in the area knew of Einstein's problems as a sailor, and there were many rescues at sea! He may have been a skilled mathematician, but apparently he was not a skilled sailor!*

# 5

## *Various Anecdotes*

Here's a cute story that points up Einstein's sense of humor.

When the Riverside Church in New York City was being built, the owners decided to put statues of the greatest scholars who ever lived over the entrance. Dr. Harry Emerson Fosdick, in order to determine who should be considered the ten greatest men, sent out requests for lists to many of the very noted scientists all over the world.

When the lists were submitted, they varied somewhat as to most of the names. However, one name was on every single list! And this was *Albert Einsten.*

It came to pass that they made these statues, which I saw, and I saw Einstein alongside Moses, Christ, Sir Isaac Newton, Galileo, Archimedes, Aristotle, Plato, and others. One evening, after having seen it, I said to Einstein, "Say, how does it feel to have your statue up there alongside Christ and Moses while you are still alive here?"

He said, "You know, I must be very careful for the rest of my life that I do not commit a scandal!" And he laughed. "This could be very embarrassing to those who chose me."

*The Juilliard School was a few streets over from the Riverside Church, and while I was attending Juilliard during 1948–50, I made it a point to visit the Church and view the statues. They created quite an impression!*

Now, here's a little example of his playfulness. Do you remember, Joan, one day he was having coffee and cake in our kitchen, and you came in with a little girl playmate of yours, and he was talking with you when I heard him ask you a question:

"If you could jump three feet high here on the earth, how high do you think you could jump if you could be on the moon?"

You didn't seem to know; and he said, "I will tell you. On the moon, you could jump eighteen feet high. How would you like to be able to do this? Wouldn't that be fun?"

Do you recall that?

*Yes, I recall that. However, it seems to me that I was sitting at the kitchen table, playing cards with my friends when Einstein approached us with the riddle. He was having dinner at our house, after having sailed from Nassau Point to Southold in his sailboat. But that is another story that you will find later in this narration.*

One time I said to him, "What are you working on at the present? I am sure you are probably engaged in some work."

And he replied, "You know, we have a good understanding of the behavior and movement of large bodies in space, and for this we have good mathematical formulas; but somehow these formulas do not work so well in the field of the minute ... that is, atoms and the particles of which they consists. And so, we are trying to formulate mathematical laws for their behavior. And you know, I find this very difficult. It is a very difficult task."

"Well," I said, "has this something to do with the Unified Field Theory that you are supposed to be working on?"

He said, "Quite so."

Dr. Einstein loved walking. We did a great deal of walking together. Always our conversation got around to our mutual craving to comprehend the nature of the universe ... to understand its meaning. As I said before, how strange it was that at the same age, each of us was so absorbed in this pursuit! He read Darwin intensely, and studied him for a long time. Always, we got around to discussing the works of Huxley, Schopenhauer and Hume, and it was a source of great satisfaction that this great man had this common interest with me. I was able to carry on this type of conversation with him for long periods of time.

One day, at the invitation of a friend of mine who was an engineer at the RCA receiving station in Riverhead, Einstein and I decided to visit the place. We started out in my car, with his son Harry along. Along the way, a salesman spotted us heading west, and since he was coming to see me at the store, he turned around and chased us. As he pulled up alongside, I pulled off the road.

"Is that Professor Einstein, Dave?" he asked. And without waiting for any response, Einstein said, "Yes, that is correct."

I gave the salesman an order for the store, and we proceeded on our course. I said to Einstein, "I hope you didn't mind being pulled off the road like that. I hope you didn't think we were being arrested."

"Oh, no," he said. "I thought nothing of this. But had this happened in Germany, I would have been very much concerned, and probably somewhat frightened."

Einstein went on to tell me that one day in Berlin, storm troopers came to his home and made him and his wife get out of the house while they were ransacking it, looking, they said, for weapons. They suddenly came running out of the house waving carving knives—ordinary carving knives—shouting, "The swine! He has weapons in the house."

"They proceeded to smash mine sailing boat, of which I was very fond, and I said to mine wife, "Look good (sic) on this place, for you shall not see it again.""

He told me that he sent word to some friends, who immediately spirited them out of the country into Belgium or Holland, and he said to me, "If they would have catched (sic) me, they would have killed me. Of that I am sure."

We proceeded on to Riverhead, and we looked the plant over. He was shown around, and seemed to be very interested. When I got near him, he was talking to the head of the place, a Dr. Bainbridge; and I heard Einstein ask him some question about the ionosphere and radio wave propagation.

Bainbridge said to him, "I can't answer that. We're not interested in the technical aspects of radio transmission here. We're only interested in the commercial angle."

And Dr. Einstein said, "Oh, but you are wrong. Without taking an interest in the theoretical aspects in this field, you would not have this beautiful station here."

I thought that was a pretty good answer!

We left and drove home, and during that half hour, we had a most fascinating discussion about so many subjects. We touched on everything ... religion, relativity, even spiritualism.

I asked him what he thought about extra-sensory perception, life-after-death, and things of that nature.

Einstein responded, "Baloney!"

I said, "But one must have an open mind. After all, what about Sir Oliver Lodge, and W.H.K. Meyers, who wrote a tremendous volume of about one thousand pages enumerating about one thousand cases of extrasensory perception for which he could not find an answer? I keep my mind open. I don't believe in it, but I'm willing to be shown. Don't you think that is correct?"

Einstein said, "Baloney!"

And the son said, "Me too! Baloney!"

In our discussion on relativity, I had some questions. It seemed to me ridiculous that one couldn't draw a straight line in space.

The son said to me, "You could not do it. You could not draw a straight line one thousand feet long in space. You could not do it. You could not do it!"

I don't remember the details ... I just remember that phrase.

Oh, we had discussed so many subjects. I wish I could remember all of them; but I just don't remember any more. Perhaps they will come to my mind later.

# 6

## *Bigraphical Background of David Arthur Rothman*

*At this point, I would like to give you some background on the life of my Dad, David Arthur Rothman. It shows how Dad became the kind of person who could have a friendship with a scientific giant like Dr. Albert Einstein, and gives some insight into that friendship.*

*I wrote most of this on November 1, 1988. The research came from my memories of what Dad had told me, and from a notebook that was in Dad's papers. Also, my mother, Ruth Rothman, did a taped interview for me in about 1985.*

*Dad made beautiful scrapbooks that showed his activities and public presentations about Einstein and Benjamin Britten. He said, "This will help you remember what kind of a person I was."*

## DAVID ARTHUR ROTHMAN

My father, David Arthur Rothman, was born on September 14, 1896, in New York City, the son of Chaim (Charles) Rothman and Baracha (Betty) Glick Rothman. Chaim was born in Warsaw, Poland, and Betty Glick was born in Miskolcz, Hungary near Budapest. They were Orthodox Jews—very devout. Chaim was a garment worker, who worked long hours for little money. The family was very poor.

This photo of Chaim Rothman, with his tallit and prayer book, illustrates his Orthodox Jewish faith:

Photo by David Rothman

There were five children in all: Morris, a girl who died at 19 months, David, Samuel, and Charles "Buster." They lived on New York's Lower East side, teeming with people and pushcarts on the stiflingly hot city streets. Baracha used to cook big pots of soup, which they used to fill up on because there was often no other food. She used to tie garlic around David's neck, to keep illness away. There were so many superstitions in those days ... but perhaps the odor kept people away and prevented illness!

Dad said that once he spilled the boiling soup all over his arm. When the arm finally healed, the entire skin peeled off like a glove. Medical care at that time was non-existent, and there were no antibiotics.

Later on, the family moved to Bayonne, New Jersey. David realized at an early age (14), that he had to work to help support the family. Samuel had polio when he was young, and couldn't walk; so the older brothers carried him everywhere on their backs. Sam became an optometrist, and when he was older, he invented the crutches that supported the upper arms. He took no money for this invention, but donated his invention for the good of mankind.

After completing the eighth grade, David left school. He had taught himself telegraphy with help from Morris, by practicing on a homemade key in his attic. He was able to obtain a job as a telegrapher on the Jersey Central Railroad. Eventually he became a tower man, controlling the paths of real trains, at an age when most boys were still playing with toy trains. Once, he was almost hit by a train when he was walking the tracks in a trance-like state. From that time on, he felt that he was living on borrowed time.

He became a stationmaster, and this is when he decided to educate himself by reading the 100 Greatest Books.

Dad had a very strong sense of justice. One day, someone came to the station and did something of which Dad disapproved. He spoke harshly to this person. It turned out that this person was someone very important ... much higher up within the company than even Dad's immediate boss. Well, the boss scolded my Dad and informed him that he must be kind and show respect for every customer, even if the customer was wrong. Dad said that really taught him an important lesson in human relations!

During this time, my mother, Ruth Samuel, was riding the train to her secretarial job each day, and she would wave to my father. Eventually they met, and after a prim and proper courtship, they married. My Dad said he'd never so much as held her hand until they were engaged! The love letters they exchanged gave me a beautiful picture of their lives at that time, because both of them described every minute of their days. They were separated when Mother went to visit Nana (Aunt Regina Sturmdorf) in Southold, or when Ruth and Nana went to Florida. Those letters were so wonderful, and revealing of their lives and love.

My parents were married on January 6, 1918. They kept a beautiful diary, which I will include in later chapters of this book.

My sister, Emma Leah Rothman (Levin), was born on May 25, 1919. At this point my parents were too busy to continue writing in the diary, and they stopped writing for many years. However, Mother began keeping the diary again starting in the 1950's, and continued until her death on May 23, 1987.

Mom and Dad decided that they didn't want to raise a family in the city, without trees and grass; so Dad gave up his lucrative job, and they sold their house, which had been given to them by Mother's father (actually they paid Grandpa $500 for it), and used the money to move to Southold, NY, and start a department store there. Everyone thought they were crazy to move to "the end of the earth" in 1919.

Dad knew nothing about business, but he decided that if he spent less than he earned, he couldn't go wrong. The store was in the center of town in Southold, on the north side of the street. About a year later, the pharmacy building on the south side of the street went on the market, so Dad bought that and moved everything into the new building. There was a house attached to the store, and that is where we lived. I still have some beautiful apothecary bottles from the pharmacy.

The store had a second story that was used for extra stock or larger items. In the area toward the street, the telephone company had its headquarters. The telephone operator took all calls, since there were no dial telephones in those days.

If there were a fire, the operator was called. Then Dad would turn on the deafeningly loud fire alarm outside on the side of the building, and the fire engines would drive past the store. Dad would stand out in front and shout out the location of the fires! I should think that many houses would have burned to the ground, with that arrangement!

Meanwhile, a second child was born, on September 28, 1922, a boy named Arthur Ozias "Buddy" Rothman. It seems that Buddy had a stomach ache one day, when he was about 6 years old. He complained to Minnie Manweiler, the telephone operator upstairs, and she gave him a laxative. That was the worst remedy for Buddy, for he actually had appendicitis. Buddy died in March, 1929, of a burst appendix and peritonitis, 1 year and 2 months before I was born. My parents never recovered from their grief. My father said that the wound was just as deep throughout his life as it was on that terrible day, when Buddy died at the age of six-and-a-half.

David Rothman taught himself to play the violin when he was 36—partly to distract himself from his grief over losing Buddy. He was helped by his brother-in-law, Milton Samuel, the professionally trained violinist.

When I was small, I used to hear my Mom and Dad making music on the piano and violin. They always had problems staying together … I think that Dad had problems with rhythm and counting!

Since Rothman's Department Store featured the latest in GE appliances, we were among the first families to have the latest inventions. Dealers were encouraged to purchase the products at reduced prices so that they could describe their advantages from experience. We had one of the first monitor top refrigerators, then later models, and even a dishwasher. We had a kitchen that was quite modern, even by today's standards, with metal cabinets and efficient work counters.

Dad was a wonderful host when celebrities came into the store. Sir Colon Davis, the British conductor, used to be a customer. Alistair Cook, the host of PBS's Masterpiece Theater came in quite often. Dad was at home with everyone.

During the years 1948–50, a theater was started in Southold, called the *Southold Playhouse.* The producer was Brett Warren, and he hired some young actors and actresses who would later become famous: Walter Matthau, Anne Meara, and Jack Warden. There wasn't much to do in Southold on quiet evenings; so usually the group would visit our home and listen to Dad's recordings. I remember their relaxing on the floor of our living room! On one evening, I played my entire Juilliard audition program on the piano. I also was hired to improvise the music for a show, "Dark of the Moon." On one occasion, I took Walter Matthau sailing in my small sailboat!

I remember the great Hurricane of 1938. This storm was totally unpredicted and unexpected. However, as the wind became stronger, Dad realized that this was a hurricane! He called the principal of the Southold High School and said,

"Mr. Blodgett, this is a hurricane! Don't let the children leave the school. Keep them there until the storm is over."

At that point, the telephone line went dead.

I remember looking out the windows of the school and watching the trees as they fell over, as the wind howled and groaned.

Finally, at around 4 P.M., we were told that we could go home. We walked, and I held onto my brother to keep from blowing away. Of course, we had no electricity for many days; and the fallen trees reminded us of that event for years. There were no chain saws in those days.

When the North Fork Concert Association was formed in about 1946 to present classical concerts on the North Fork, Dad was on the board and helped select the performers.

Many years later, Dad was proud to have played the violin in the pit orchestra for "Jesus Christ, Superstar."

Dad enjoyed his children very much, especially my brother Bob. (Dad said that girls were okay, but there was nothing like a man having a *son*.) When we were very young, Mom and Dad took us on trips to New York to see shows, occasionally. (It seemed to take forever to get there!) Every New Year's Eve during those years, we would stay at the Hotel Taft and watch the ball dropping at midnight.

When I broke up with a boyfriend at the age of 13, I was very upset. Dad tried to console me. He told me how he had had a girlfriend whom he wanted to marry; but she refused, because she was much older than Dad. Dad said, "I was devastated, but what if I had married her? Then I wouldn't have married your mother, and it would have been a disaster!"

In 1939, my mother had a mental collapse. It was while she was recovering that Dad met Albert Einstein. In 1939 he also met Benjamin Britten and Peter Pears. They were young, not too well known, broke, and discouraged at that time. They had come to the United States because a friend had told them that in America, homosexuals were more accepted than they were in England. However, I also read that they came as conscientious objectors, to escape World War II in England. In addition, the English government wished to protect their great public assets, an English composer and a great tenor. This composer later became a Peer, and his works are now performed all over the world.

When Britten and Pears were on the ship coming to the United States, they became friends with Dr. William Mayer and his wife, Elizabeth Mayer. Dr. William Mayer was my mother's psychiatrist at the sanitarium in Amityville. Since Britten and Pears had no place to stay, they lived with the Mayer's for some time.

Dad helped Britten and Pears in their careers by entertaining them, finding work for them, and encouraging them. My Dad was interviewed many years later for a film about Britten, "A Time There Was ... An Intimate Portrait of Benjamin Britten," made by the BBC in England. The entire BBC camera crew came to Southold to interview and film Dad in his living room. Dad and the family were invited to the premier in New York, where we met Aaron Copland and Leonard Bernstein. It was a proud moment.

I remember Dad shaking hands with Aaron Copland. He said, "This is a very special hand, because it shook the hand of Albert Einstein!"

Copland seemed quite amused by that.

I performed the Copland *Violin Sonata* with Max Pollikoff, who conducted the *Music in Our Time* series at the YMCA in New York City during the 1950's. I did have another occasion to meet Aaron Copland, when the two-piano team of Gold and Fizdale performed his two-piano composition at Guild Hall in East Hampton. (I was program chairman of the Music Committee, and there was a reception after the concert.)

Dad would never acknowledge the fact that Britten and Pears had a homosexual relationship. Quite recently, we learned of Britten's interest in young boys.

A few years ago, my brother Bob and his wife Audrey visited Great Britain. They visited Aldeburg, and Bob and Aud went to the office and inquired about the location of Britten's home.

"Why do you want to know that?" asked the directors.

My brother replied, "Ben invited me there many years ago. I'm a little late, but I'd like to visit the home."

"But who *are* you?" Bob was asked.

Bob explained who he was, and was given a grand welcome and much attention. He was invited to a reception, too. Later, he learned why he was given such a grand welcome, and what a surprise *that* was!

It seems that there was a theory that Britten was in love with my brother! We never knew that Britten had many young boys for companions. The boys were later abandoned rudely, when they became older. There's even a video, interviewing some of Britten's boys.

Bob said that Britten never made any sexual advances toward him, even though they slept in twin beds in the same room! Bob is married and has three sons. He is completely normal. He says, even now, that he was unaware of Britten's love for him until the recent incident in England.

However, my Juilliard roommate in 1949, the soprano Phyllis Antognini, found a song that Britten dedicated to Bob. Bob asked Britten why he hadn't told him about the song. Britten said that he didn't want to embarrass Bob; so it seems that the theory was true. (Bob doesn't seem to remember that Phyllis had discovered the song so many years ago.) That's probably why Britten wanted to give up music and go to work in Dad's store! Dad talked Britten out of that.

Recent publications about the life of Benjamin Britten discuss Ben's attraction to young boys, and his attraction to young Bobby.[1]

At any rate, Britten and my Dad were great friends. One day, probably during the summer of 1940, the entire family went on a picnic in Hither Hills, on the South Fork of Long Island, near Montauk. I missed the picnic because I had gone with Nana and my cousin, Janice Loeb, on a trip in the old Buick. We drove to Riverhead.

Mom and Dad didn't want me to know about the picnic because they knew I'd be heartbroken at having missed it. However, Dad took movies of the event, with all sitting at the wooden picnic table having a wonderful time!

My sister Emma was there, as well as Bobby, Ben, Dad and Mother.

Dad also took movies of Britten at one of the beaches, and there were flocks of seagulls flying about, darting hither and yon. When BBC filmed the show about Britten and interviewed Dad in Southold, Dad showed them the movies. The BBC asked to borrow the films, which they did. When the films were finally returned to Dad, after much reminding from him, Dad felt that some of the footage was missing.

There were times when Britten stayed at our house in Southold when he wanted to work at his composing.

Dad said, "We have many places here that will inspire you to compose … the beaches, the forests … I'll be happy to give you a tour."

Britten replied that he needed only a chair, a table, and manuscript paper. He didn't even need the piano, for he heard all of the sounds in his head, before he notated them on paper.

Later in life, Britten and Dad lost touch with each other. As time passed, Dad never heard from Britten, although he followed Britten's career avidly.

Then Britten was invited to conduct his Requiem in the United States. He contacted Dad and said that someone had told him about a gentleman in Southold who was very interested in his career.

It seems that Britten had had surgery, and while the operation was in progress, the electricity failed. The generator didn't work, and Britten had sustained brain damage. Apparently, that's why he had forgotten Dad.

---

1. See *February House* by Sherrill Tippens

However, gradually his memories of Southold came back. He invited Dad to the concert, but Dad couldn't attend. Britten sent Dad a score to the Requiem that I still possess.

I must mention here that I once had a piano lesson from Britten. I was studying the Chopin *Fantasie-Impromptu Opus 66* at the time, and it was a very difficult work. There was one passage that I missed each time that I had to play it, and it is repeated about four times during this beautiful composition. Well, finally Ben couldn't stand listening to it! He approached me at the piano and said, "Let's hear you play that *slowly*!"

I tried, but I couldn't play the passage slowly. I said, "I can't play it slowly. I can only play it fast!"

Ben replied, "Well, if you can't play it slowly, you can't play it fast!"

Truer words were never spoken, and I'll never forget that lesson!

I have a lovely letter from Benjamin Britten written in about 1941. In it, Britten mentions a work that he had just composed for two pianos and orchestra. He describes playing it in a piano store with the two-piano team of Bartlett and Robinson, with Britten playing the orchestra part on a third piano.

Here is a copy of my letter:

> Escondido, California
>
> Sept. 15ᵗʰ 1941
>
> Dear Joan,
>
> Please forgive me for not having answered your nice letter before, but, as you can guess, I have been just as busy as possible these last few months, and the only kind of letters I have been able to write have been horrible business ones!
>
> Anyhow, thank you very much for it. I was very interested to hear about your doings at camp. You seem to have had a swell time, and done some exciting things. I am glad you avoided being 'dunked' in the lake — that sounds very unpleasant! I have had a nice time out here — I have worked very hard, but also had some nice trips

You will notice that he mentions the Chopin Op. 66!

> is the ocean (with swimming) and into the mountains all around, which are very high and beautiful.
>
> I have just written a piece for 2 pianos and orchestra which Bartlett & Robertson, the piano-duo, who are our hosts here, are going to play next season. The other day we went to a music store and played it on 3 pianos (I played the orchestral part on another piano) — you cannot imagine how much noise we all made banging away together. How was the composing contest? — and how is the 'Fantasie-Impromptu' coming along?
>
> Give my love to all the family, including that 'rapscallion' of a brother of yours — if he knows what that means! And lots of luck to you this term at school.
>
> Your friend,
> Benjamin Britten

*Bigraphical Background of David Arthur Rothman* 33

## ENGLAND'S FIRST MUSICAL PEER

This article appeared on June 13, 1976 in Newsday. It was so faded that I am retyping it to make it legible:

Benjamin Britten, England's foremost composer, became a lord yesterday when Queen Elizabeth II published her traditional midyear Honors List. Britten, 62, the first person elevated to the peerage for musical achievement, composed choral works, song cycles and operas, including "Peter Grimes", the first English opera to win foreign acclaim in 300 years, when it was first performed in 1945.

Edward Elgar and William Walton, Brittain's other two leading composers of recent times, both were knighted. The queen also knighted Douglas Bader, 66, who lost both legs in a 1933 air crash but managed to re-enter the Royal Air Force to fly in the Battle of Britain in 1940 and become an ace. Bader shot down 22 German planes before he was captured after a collision over occupied France in 1944. He has become a symbol of hope for Britain's disabled.

Compiled from Newsday Reports. June 13, 1976.

In upper left-hand corner, hand-written by Britten: " To the Rothmans. Affectionately, Benjamin Britten" .

Britten and Pears were in the United States during 1939–1942. When Britten died on December 4, 1976, Dad was very upset. I tried to comfort him, but Dad wouldn't be comforted.

Of course Dad was devastated when Einstein died in 1955. I remember his telling me that Einstein had refused all major medical efforts to extend his life when he became ill. He just wanted to die in peace. After Einstein's death, the doctors realized that any heroic efforts would not have helped; so Einstein was spared much pain and grief. My father felt the same way about his own life and death.

Dad had many interests in addition to music and reading. He also enjoyed boating, crabbing, fishing, nature, photography, art, astronomy, ballroom dancing, and science. Dad had his own darkroom, and printed and edited his own wonderful photos. I appreciated his vast education only when I attended college myself as an adult. (It's difficult to believe, but Dad once told me that he had practiced *boxing* with Morris when he was a young man!)

Dad purchased, from a friend, a telescope that had been salvaged from the sailing ship, "Resolute," that had sailed from the New York Yacht Club in 1887. It was engraved with the names of the shipmates and Captain, but it was in terrible shape. Dad restored that beautiful instrument, and now I have it in my living room:

Dad said that the educated man understood man and his relationship to the universe. A college education meant nothing if one missed a true understanding of the nature of man. The educated man could speak for a day about a blade of grass. Education helped one live a useful, satisfying life. Goodness was its own reward. Man was partly the product of his heredity, but mostly of his environment. Dad took most of the credit for my piano playing!

My Dad had little use for organized religion, for he felt that it divided the world, rather than unifying the world. He was in favor of one universal religion. He often said that if you took all of the money and effort which went into building churches and used it to relieve world suffering, you could work wonders. Religion too often resulted in prejudice and bigotry, and even war. However, he appreciated the long tradition of Judaism and did what he could to help it survive in the small community in which he lived. He did his share, even though we were the only Jewish family in Southold for many, many years.

I was very proud when we walked together or when he gave me special attention. I treasure the lovely gifts he presented me with: pearl earrings; an alexandrite pendant from Jerusalem; some beautiful Indian jewelry; Chanel No. 5 perfume; a Comet sailboat; a Lorée oboe; and a Steinway piano. He also helped me remodel my home in East Hampton, and paid for my divorce in 1976.

Dad also recorded this Einstein story for me, which is a *great* gift!

When Dad was about 70, he and mother took dance lessons. On most Saturday evenings, they would go out for dinner and dancing. Mom and Dad won many bottles of champagne with their dancing ... especially when they did the Cha-Cha!

Dad loved his work in the store—Rothman's Department Store—and loved having my brother, and later his grandson, Ronnie Rothman, in the store helping him. He loved to fix things, and take care of his family. He nursed Mother through her many illnesses.

Dad was a vegetarian for many years. He "ate to live" and not vice versa. He tried to live healthfully. However, in the 1960's, both Mother and Dad were operated on for colon cancer, although Mother never knew that her tumor was malignant. They both recovered and lived more than 25 years after their surgeries. When we gave Dad advice on health, he would say, "I must be doing something right ... and I can't die young anymore!"

David A. Rothman lived a long, useful life, and was much loved by all who knew him. He took a personal interest in all his customers, and I've heard many tales from those whom he helped. He had a whimsical sense of humor. My parents were married for over 63 1/2 years, and they were entirely devoted, as couples rarely are today. My Dad worshipped my mother—and she worshipped him. Dad called my Mom "One in a million ..." As life progressed, they looked forward to each day together. Every morning, Dad would say, "Well, we have another day together."

Occasionally, Dad would become very angry about something. Once Mother gave a gentleman a kiss on the cheek, to thank him for some kindness. Dad was furious! It was several days before Dad calmed down again. Mother wrote about this in one of her notebooks.

However, Dad did tell me once that it was always *he* who had to apologize, not mother. Mother never apologized to Dad!

In David Rothman's later years, he was interviewed by Columbia University for their "living history" library-on-tape. I believe that Dad spoke about his work on the Jersey Central Railroad. I have been unable to locate that tape. He was also invited to speak to many groups about Einstein and Britten, including groups of college science professors.

In Dad's later life, he decided to study art. He obtained a large collection of reproductions of great artworks, and could identify most of the great artists of the past, up to the present day.

I think of my father's life as a great American story. Born to immigrant parents, living in poverty on the teeming tenement streets of Manhattan on the lower East Side, he was forced to end his formal education at the age of 14, in order to work to help his family. But such was his thirst for knowledge and self-improvement that he fashioned an intense course of reading great works of philosophy and science. This established, along with his love of music, the basis of a unique and lasting friendship with a great man, when fate brought him together with one of the giants of our age.

David Rothman died on November 19, 1981, of acute leukemia.

# 7

## *My Mother Ruth Samuel Rothman*

Ruth Samuel Rothman was born in on October 20, 1898 in New York City, the daughter of Joseph Samuel (b. 1860) and Emma Noé Samuel (b. 1860). There were three brothers and five sisters in Mother's family. Joseph manufactured fur coats and was quite wealthy by standards of that day.

The children were: Hermine, Florence ("Flossie"), Herbert, David, Milton, Mabel, Ruth and Jeanette. They were two years apart, except that there were five years between Mabel and Ruth, and 6 years between Ruth and Jeanette.

I gather that Grandpa Joseph was quite strict, but loving. Mother said that he was born in Germany ... actually Prussia, which was alternately controlled by Germany and Poland. Grandpa came to the United States in around 1877 in order to avoid being conscripted into the army. During that era, all young men were expected to become part of the army to protect the country. Grandpa spoke German and English, and I think that he also spoke Polish.

My grandmother, Emma Noé Samuel, was one of two sisters (actually half sisters, I think), born in Paris, France. They lived in Paris with their mother, Johanna Elbe Noé. The latter studied for the opera and then became a seamstress for Sarah Bernhardt, among others. The father, Louis Noé, was not mentioned, as far as I know, except on some legal papers, and I don't know why. My dad suspected that Regina and Johanna were illegitimate because there was so little mention of their father. Perhaps Johanna Noé was a courtesan, as was Sarah Bernhardt.

However, the Noé family was educated in music and languages—Regina spoke five languages fluently: English, French, German, Italian, and Yiddish. They were "refined." Therefore, Emma's marriage to Joseph was not very happy, for Joseph was a plain man, and the two were very different in temperament and education.

Ruth and Jeanette were very close, being the youngest. When Ruth was 12 and Jeanette was 7, Emma Noé Samuel died (in 1910) after being in a sanitarium for some time. Joseph later married Lina, my step-grandmother.

It was only at that time that Mother learned about her Aunt Regina. Apparently, Emma and Regina had been estranged when Regina married Dr. Arnold Sturmdorf, a famous gynecologist, with whom Emma had been in love. It seems that both Emma and Regina played the piano, and Dr. Sturmdorf played the violin. Emma and Regina took turns accompanying the doctor, but Regina married him! After that, the two half-sisters had no contact.

Regina had no children of her own. After Emma Noé died, Regina wanted to adopt Jeanette or Ruth, but not both of them. Joseph would not agree to this. So Jeanette and Ruth took turns visiting Aunt Regina in Southold, L.I., where she had a beautiful summer home. Eventually Regina and her husband were divorced, after 27 years of marriage, when, I believe, Dr. Sturmdorf fell in love with his nurse. Divorce in those days was considered scandalous; but then, Regina was a rebel who refused to ride side-saddle and spelled words according to their sound, and the way she tho't they should be spelled. I called Regina "Nana," but she was really my great-aunt. She drove her own car and swam in Long Island Sound when she was in her seventies. It is hard to believe that Nana was 68 when I was born! She died in 1951, when I was pregnant with my first child, Shelley Jo Brill.

Nana was a fine pianist and also sang in the New York Choral Society under Walter Damrosch. She wrote letters to many famous people, and the letters were so interesting that the people would answer her! Thus, I have her entire autograph collection, and also the correspondence she had with Benjamin Britten. Apparently Britten was very fond of Nana.

Nana had little use for my father because he was not "refined." However, I worshipped Nana—she was my role model, as was my father. It was due to Nana's influence that Mom and Dad decided to move to Southold. Southold was the only place out in the country with which they were familiar. In 1919 the trip must have taken at least a day. It was "the other end of the world."

I always sensed antagonism between Dad and Nana. When I asked my Mom about it, she said that after she married Dad, Nana still tried to boss her around and tell her how to do everything. Mother finally told Nana that now she was grown up and needed to live her own life. I guess that Nana never forgave my Mom. She didn't remember Mother in her will. Nana gave everything to Jeanette, even though it was my Mom who cared for Nana when she was ill, and stayed with her until she died. Mother was very hurt by that. It wasn't that

Mother wanted the money; but she would have appreciated some remembrance. Jeanette did give Mother some of Nana's beautiful objects ... a teak table with a marble top, and a beautiful vase.

I received Nana's very old Steinway upright piano. The piano is still in my living room, and will hopefully be enjoyed by my musical grandchildren.

Nana gave me some of her treasures when I graduated from Southold High School as Valedictorian, with the highest average in the history of the school. One such treasure was a beautiful antique necklace with semi-precious stones. She also gave me the opera glasses that I still use today.

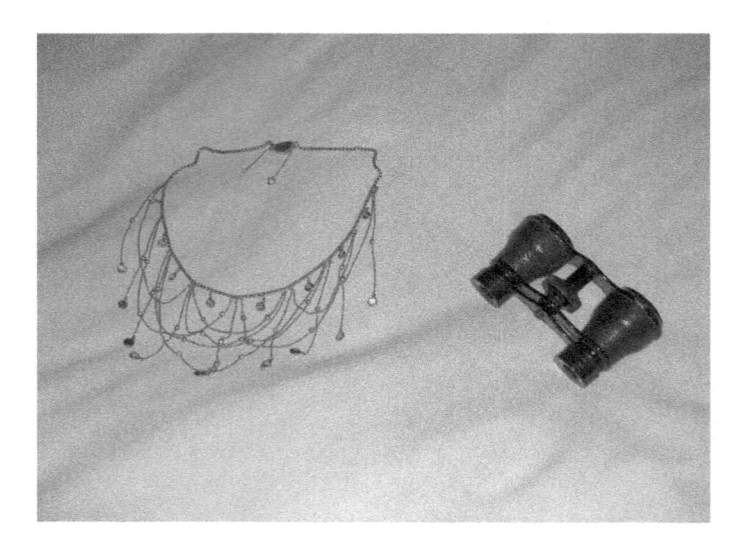

My mother was extremely devoted to her family. I remember our walks in the woods, and how she showed me the ospreys and the trailing arbutus. She took us to the beach to swim every nice day of each summer until I was quite grown up.

Mother was very philosophical about life, accepting the happy and sad times as they occurred. We had so many beautiful family dinners. In about 1938 Mother had 22 people for a Seder at the house. Grandpa Samuel conducted the ceremony.

Mother enjoyed sewing and crafts. She did tatting, and knitted and crocheted, and made many fine braided rugs, which today adorn my home and the homes of my children, nieces, and nephews. Here is a photo of one of the best, beautiful, large rugs:

Mother sang, and played the piano. When I was young, she would sing for me, accompanying herself on the piano. She told me that years before, she had often played background music on the piano for silent films at the local movie theaters. Her early piano lessons were $.50 each, and usually the teacher would go into another room while mother was playing. She suspected that the teacher was sleeping! (When I started giving lessons in East Hampton in 1950, I charged $4.00 a lesson.)

Mother was plagued by recurring mental illness from clinical depression, which apparently was hereditary in some members of the Samuel-Noé family. (Sister Hermine committed suicide.) However, Mother also lived a long, useful life, contributing much to her family and community.

In 1939, Mother had a serious illness that was diagnosed as the flu. She had a high fever and became delirious. She was given Phenobarbital for sedation; but the more of the drug she took, the worse she became.

Finally, Mother was taken to the sanitarium in Amityville, NY. She was treated by the psychiatrist, Dr. William Mayer. Mother was given very little chance of recovery because, in those days, there was no cure for mental illness.

Dad became a good friend of Dr. Mayer and his wife, Elizabeth. (Elizabeth was a translator of the works of Goethe from German to English.) Both had come over from Germany on the same ship with the budding composer, Benjamin Britten, and Peter Pears, a great English tenor. Britten and Pears lived with the Mayer's because they had no place else to stay.

Often, the Mayer's would send Britten and Pears to Southold to visit with us, just to give them a change. They needed work, so Dad arranged for Pears to conduct the Southold Choral Society, while Britten became the accompanist. I remember attending the rehearsals with my mother, who sang with the Choral Society. I fell in love with the Alexander Borodin *Polovtsian Dances* from the opera *Prince Igor*. When they presented this work in concert, the accompanists were Britten and Colin McPhee, on two pianos!

Dad also helped found a Symphony Orchestra in Southampton, NY that Britten conducted. Natalie Boshko Brown was soloist in the Brusch Violin Concerto.

Here is the announcement of *The Suffolk Friends of Music Orchestra*, printed in 1941:

## The Suffolk Friends of Music Orchestra

**Season 1941**

**BENJAMIN BRITTEN, Conductor**

**BENJAMIN BRITTEN**
Conductor

The Suffolk Friends of Music announce with pride the engagement of the noted English composer, pianist and conductor, Benjamin Britten, as their conductor. A graduate of the Royal College of Music, the London Daily Telegraph speaks of him as "unquestionably the most brilliant of the younger British composers." Though he is now but 27 years old, his compositions have been featured by the major festivals of England and the Continent. In the United States, Britten compositions have been performed by Albert Stoessel's Chatauqua Orchestra, Wallenstein's WOR Sinfonietta, and the New York Philharmonic Orchestra, under Barbirolli. Mr. Britten's new "Sintonia da Requiem" will be played by the New York Philharmonic on March 29 and 30, 1941.

As conductor, Mr. Britten has appeared with the British Broadcasting Company Orchestra, the London Philharmonic and the London Symphony, and also has spent a period as conductor of the English government film project.

### A Symphony Orchestra in Suffolk County

The Suffolk Friends of Music Orchestra is composed of three types of players: professional musicians, adult amateurs, and advanced students of high school age. All volunteer their services in the orchestra for the sole reward of establishing in Suffolk a permanent symphony orchestra, sincere in its musical purpose, and aiming high in artistic achievment.

Attracting new players with each rehearsal, the Orchestra numbered forty-five players in December, 1940. Concerts are planned for the months of March and April in Southampton, Riverhead, Port Jefferson and Amityville.

### The Musical Advisory Board

The Musical Advisory Board consists of several internationally prominent musicians who indorse the work of the SUFFOLK FRIENDS OF MUSIC ORCHESTRA. Some are residents of Suffolk. They are as follows:

DOUGLAS MOORE, Chairman, Head of Music Department of Columbia College; Cutchogue and New York.
NATHALIE BOSHKO, Concert Violinist, Southampton and New York.
VICTOR HARRIS, Composer, East Hampton and New York.
PHILLIP JAMES, Head of Music Department, New York University; Amagansett and New York.
HARWOOD SIMMONS, Director of Columbia University Concert Band and the New York City Symphonic Band.
SIGMUND SPAETH, Author, Lecturer and Composer.

### Officers of the Suffolk Friends of Music Orchestra

PRESIDENT ............................................................ Jack Van Brederode
HONORARY PRESIDENT ................................................. Jesse Lillywhite
VICE-PRESIDENT & BUSINESS MANAGER ........... Walter Potter
SECRETARY ......................................... Donald Barth, Riverhead, N. Y.
TREASURER ........................................ Milton Samuel, Mattituck, N. Y.
PUBLICITY COMMITTEE ........ Howard Lee Koch, Anne Vojvoda
LIBRARIANS ......... Jack Cushman, Robert Richard, Thomas Stark

REGIONAL CHAIRMEN:
Bellport, Donald Baggs; Bridgehampton, Charles Mockler; Center Moriches, Chester Osborne; East Hampton, Molly Smith; Hampton Bays, John Knapp; Mattituck, Walter Williams; Port Jefferson, Jesse Van Brederode; Riverhead, Howard Hovey; Southampton, Jesse Lillywhite; Southold, David Rothman.

### Associate Memberships

The Orchestra has already received several donations from music lovers who have heard of its development. This has led to the establishment of The Associate Members of the Suffolk Friends of Music. In appreciation of this support, a private chamber music recital will be given for these associate members and the regular members of the orchestra at the close of the concert season in May. Featuring prominent soloists, the recital will be held in the new Nathalie Boshko Studio, Artist Colony, Southampton.

The Suffolk Friends of Music Orchestra solicits the Associate Membership of all who are interested in a permanent symphony orchestra in Suffolk County.

---

I wish to become an ASSOCIATE MEMBER of the SUFFOLK FRIENDS OF MUSIC. Enclosed please find my contribution for $ ..............................

---

(Associate Memberships, One Dollar or more, payable to Milton Samuel, Treasurer, Mattituck, L. I.)

It was during this time that Benjamin Britten and Peter Pears visited our home, as described in the last chapter.

At any rate, Dad was determined that Mother would recover from her illness. He brought her back home in 1940, and nursed her back to health. That's why Mother was not around when Dad spent the summer with Albert Einstein, Benjamin Britten, Peter Pears, and others.

During that year, my sister, Emma Rothman Levin left Rider College in Trenton, NJ, where she was studying to be a secretary, and came back to Southold to cook and take care of the family. She had good grades at college, so she graduated without taking the final exams.

Mother did regain her health. She had a relapse during the 1950's, during menopause. But during most of the time after that, she was fine.

Then, in her 80's, Mother had another relapse. She was given lithium, and that helped her for the rest of her life. She would try to cut down on the medication, but that always caused problems.

It was only after my father died that my mother came into her own and showed her true strength. When the store was robbed, it was my mother who urged my brother to keep calm! She held the family together and reveled in her 3 children, 7 grandchildren, and 4 great-grandchildren (4 more were born after mother's death).

In January, 1987, we learned that Mother had multiple myeloma, or cancer of the bone marrow. She said that she did not want heroic measures to keep her alive. We arranged for 24 hour care so that Mother could remain at home. On Mother's Day, all of the children and grandchildren and great-grandchildren visited, including 4 week old Gregory Dove Rothman. Mother held court in her nightgown and robe, and posed for photos. However, after that her condition steadily deteriorated, and she died under hospice care on May 23, 1987. I was with her.

# 8

# *A Diary of Love and Marriage*

*On January 6, 1918, my parents, Ruth Samuel Rothman and David Arthur Rothman were married. As they began a new life together, they also initiated "Our Diary".... personal notes in a typical school-type notebook of the day. Perhaps you will remember the black-and-white cardboard covers, with the lined pages inside. Unfortunately, the paper was not acid-free archival bond, and today most of it is crumbling. Before the diary self-destructed, I copied it so that I could include it in this book.*

*Mother and Dad always told us about the diary; and after they both died, we found it up on a shelf in the guest room. I'm sure that they would have been proud and delighted to share it with all who would enjoy reading it!*

*I will present here some highlights from the diary, for it is rather long!*

Below is a reproduction of the first page of the Diary that Mother and Dad so lovingly kept during the early days of their marriage. What beautiful handwriting! Mother continued writing until 1961.

### Our Diary

#### Foreword

On a warm summer evening, just about the time that those wonderfully cool and refreshing breezes arrive from no one knows where to furnish delightful relief to so many suffering human beings who must swelter on hot sunny days, my dearest pal, my wife, and I went out on the streets for a little stroll. I cannot exactly recall how it all came about, but we decided that after all, the human memory could not store all the treasures and sacred memories so rapidly piling up during such a happy existence as ours; and we found that we forget many things that we would remember — hence do we commence "Our Diary"

D.A.R.

May there always be nothing but happiness as we wade thru these pages, so that in years to coming, may see out our happy and full life as it should be.

# Our Diary

**FOREWORD:**

On a warm summer evening, just about the time that those wonderfully cool and refreshing breezes arrive from no one knows where, to furnish delightful relief to so many suffering human beings who must swelter on hot summer days, my dearest pal, my wife, and I went out on the streets for a little stroll. I cannot exactly recall how it all came about, but we decided that after all, the human memory could not store all the treasures and sacred memories so rapidly piling up during such a happy existence as ours; and we found that we forget many things that we would remember—hence do we commence "Our Diary."

*DAR*

May there always be nothing but happiness as we wade thru these pages, so that in years to come we may see our own happy and full life as it should be.

*Ruth*

This is a photo of the Samuel family, many of whom are mentioned in the diary. Front, seated: Herbert Samuel, Stepmother Lina Samuel, Ruth Samuel Rothman, Milton Samuel, Flossie Samuel Ravitz Linde (whose mother died in childbirth).

Rear, standing: Jeanette Samuel Loeb Dennis, Mabel Samuel Weinberg, Bernice and Harriet Samuel (David's daughters), Stanley Samuel (Herbert's son), Hermine Samuel Levin, David Samuel

*A Diary of Love and Marriage*     49

Photo by Joan Rothman Brill
This is a 1947 photo of Regina Noé Sturmdorf, whom I called "Nana." She was my mother's Aunt. Nana was a great influence on my life ... a pianist, musician, and role-model. She is mentioned a great deal in the diary to follow.

## Saturday, August 17, 1918

*(This is Dad writing. I am trying to retain the language and spelling that was in the diary, so if it seems odd, that will be the reason.)* Rec'd word the previous night that I would have to report for duty at 4 a.m. I worked until noon and for the first time in a very long time, I had dinner at noon at home with my wife. After dinner I invited my wife to take a trip with me but I had thought of nowhere in particular to go to. We finally decided on a trip to East New York to visit my relatives. When we arrived there, we found most of them to be away from home. A few minutes after we got there, however, I was very agreeably surprised by the sudden appearance of my Cousin Eddie, whom I had not seen in a few years. He arrived from a trip thru New England with a three-seater Mitchell auto. After we enjoyed some milk, fruit and cakes, Eddie invited us out for a trip in his car. He drove us to Coney Island—along a very picturesque road thru Prospect Park, Brooklyn, and the pretty scenes I feel sure have impressed themselves firmly and vividly on our memory. Returning from Coney Island, we stopped at a very spacious sort of pavilion and had beer and frankfurters on rolls, which we enjoyed very much. After our return to East New York, we enjoyed a nice meal and waited until the bunch returned. My absent relatives returned about ten P.M. and after a short talk we started for home; coming all the way to NY in Eddie's car. Cousin Eva *(Atkins)* gave us a plant which we brought home with us. (*Eva Atkins was part of the Atkins family who owned a flower shop.*) Reached Bayonne and "Home Sweet Home" about midnight.

*(Mom and Dad were living in Bayonne, NJ when they were first married. Dad was exempt from service in the armed forces because his job with the Jersey Central Railroad was considered essential. All this took place during WWI.)*

All in all it was a wonderful day for us both, and we enjoyed it immensely, as everything had turned out so unexpectedly and unlooked for. And after all, isn't that the best way?

I feel sure, we both feel greatly indebted to Cousin Eddie for his part in furnishing us this "Pleasant Memory."

D.

*It is interesting to note that in 2007, David and Ruth's great grandchildren are living in Brooklyn. Orin Robert Kurtz is a New York lawyer who lives near Prospect Park; and Nathania Jayne Kurtz lives in Brooklyn and works at Coney Island Hospital as an LMSW (Licensed Master of Social Work). Small world!*

## Sunday, August 18, 1918

I worked from 7 am to 4 pm. My wife met me at the railroad station. We went over to the folks' house and brought our papers, bank books, bonds etc. over to our home. Spent the evening in the parlor. To bed early.

## Monday, August 19

After supper my wife and I strolled around to the bank and opened our first checking account. Gee, but didn't it make us feel good. Felt we were coming up in the world. I was just telling my wife jokingly that maybe some day, after we had become very, very wealthy, we would laugh when we read this—about our first little bank account of $125.00.

To bed early.

## Tuesday, August 20, 1918

After supper we went to the Bayonne Opera House and enjoyed a splendid performance. It consisted of some high class vaudeville and a moving picture—Douglas Fairbanks in "Mr. Fixit." We visited my folks before going to the Opera House.

## Wednesday, August 21

This was a quiet day. Spent the evening in the parlor with my dearest—and as we sat there in the glow of the lamp, enjoying the breeze that came in thru the windows, home felt like *home* more than ever.

## Thursday, August 22

Quiet day. After supper, went around the corner to the ice-cream parlor and enjoyed some ice-cream. Met Moe Weinberg. *(Moe married mother's older sister Mabel.)* Invited him upstairs, sat in the parlor for a short time, and after Moe W. left, went to bed early.

## Friday, August 23, 1918

After supper we went to the Opera House and enjoyed a good performance. Some vaudeville and a picture—"How Could You, Jean?" with Mary Pickford. Had a very pleasant walk all the way home, for it was a wonderful night, with the moon shining exceptionally clear and bright and the heavens lit with the sharp rays of some distant searchlights, probably belonging to some far away battleships. It is on such nights as these, while walking with my wife, that I realize and feel what a happy existence I am, and have been, leading.

## Saturday, August 24

Visited the ice-cream parlor after supper. Took a short stroll during which we decided to start this diary. I have been writing since 8 o'clock. My darling lies on the sofa reading. Cool refreshing breezes pour thru the open windows. My girlie is drowsy and so am I. So I put my pen aside, turn the lamp low, and so ends another happy day.

## Sunday, August 25

This day we spent in a rather unusual way. We got out of bed around 9 am. We decided to take a trip to Philadelphia simply to look the place over. The scenery which we observed from the train as we passed thru the country was wonderful in its splendour (sic) and we both feel that the pictures of nature we saw will be long remembered. The train ride would have been ever so much more pleasant had it not been that the train struck and snuffed out the life of a poor laborer who had been working on the tracks. I prevented my wife from seeing the body as it lay crushed on the tracks, but I, being more used to such things by nature of my railroad experience, looked out of the car window and saw the body being picked up and placed on a stretcher.

We both felt quite distressed for quite some time after this sad accident, but this soon wore off, as we are the kind who try to be happy under almost any conditions. When we arrived in Philadelphia we spent most of the time walking around thru the streets, which proved very interesting to us both. We visited Independence Hall, saw the Liberty Bell, and all the other national treasures which are stored there. We reached home about 9 o'clock feeling quite tired as we both had walked a great deal and besides, my darling had not been feeling very well—during most of the day. I forgot to mention above that one of the interesting things we saw in Philadelphia was a large flock of pigeons which frequented the City Hall building and which were so tame that they would jump up on the arms of the onlookers and eat things from out of their hands.

## Monday. August 26

We just spent a quiet evening at home and as we always do, enjoyed it as much as a good show. Flossie *(Florence Samuel Ravitz, another of Mother's older sisters)* came over, and we had a nice long chat as she had just come back from Southold.

Minnie came earlier in the day and I had a great time reading our love letters to her. To bed about 9:30 P.M.

## Tuesday, August 27th

*(This is written in Mother's handwriting.)*

Felt better today so went over to see Ruth. (*I don't know who this Ruth was, with the same first name as my mother.*) Sophie was there and I was glad to see her. Mother Rothman came in the evening and we went out with her and left her at 26th Street, where we went to the Opera House. Punk show. After the show we went to buy something for my darling's lunch and after we had everything bot, we discovered that we hadn't enuf (sic) money to pay for it and had some time about it coming home. My Sweetheart teased me all the way home. To bed about 10 P.M.

## Wednesday, August 28

Was a quiet day. Spent the evening at home and we also went over to my in-laws' for a little while before retiring.

## Thursday, August 29th

*(This is in Mother's handwriting.)*

My tho'ts (sic) are my own today and to write them would spoil our diary of the weaving of dreams. And so, dear little book, as we bo't you for pleasant memories, this day shall be forgotten.

## Friday, August 30

*(Still Mother's writing.)*

We're at Mother Rothman's for supper. Came home after eating and lifted the cloud over our little home. Didn't sleep more than three hours during the last 36 hours so my nerves were pretty much on edge. And as this "saying" comes back to me I have adopted it as a mascot and motto: "There's nothing ill can dwell in such a temple.

If the ill spirit have so fair a house,
Good things will strive to dwell within it."
*(Nana always said, "Never go to bed angry!")*

## Saturday, August 31st, 1918

I went to the market in the morning and ironed when I cam home. In the afternoon, Hermine *(the oldest sister)* came up with Emeline *(Hermine's daughter)* and they stayed for supper. In the evening we went to Jersey City, intending to go to Keith's but there were no seats left so we ended by going to the Majestic Theater and saw one of the best Burlesque shows ever produced! My darling enjoyed it so much he was almost sick from laughing. It rained when we came home but we managed to keep pretty dry. To bed at 1 A.M.

## Sunday, September 1st, 1918

We arose at about 10 A.M., had our dinner right away and Dave went to work at 1 P.M. In the afternoon Flossie and I went to Cooper's, and after taking a walk to the park, went back to Cooper's for supper. Spent a very pleasant evening there and went to bed at 10 P.M. Honey came home at 10:30 P.M.

## Monday, September 2, 1918 *(Labor Day)*

Watched the parade and then went to Mother's for dinner. In the afternoon we met Hermine and Jake *(Levin)* on the 2:11 P.M. train and met Dave in Jersey City. Went to the cemetery. Then went to 42nd Street, NY, walked around and then came home. Had supper and sat in the parlor until 10 P.M. when Floss left and we went to bed.

## Tuesday, September 3

In the evening we entertained Mr. E. Sobel and Pearl Cooper for dinner and certainly had a very pleasant evening. They left about 10 P.M. and we went to bed.

## Wednesday, September 4

*(Dad's writing)*: Was obliged to work from 7 a.m. until 10:30 p.m. on this day. My dearest came down to the office with my supper and stayed with me until it was time to go home. We caught the 10:40 P.M. train and were in bed by 11:30. I enjoyed my wife's company at the office immensely and it made the time pass quickly, so that I did not mind the long day I had worked. My girlie spent the time writing to Aunt Regina. She also knitted for a while.

## Thursday, September 6, 1918

A quiet day, but a happy one. Went to Synagogue in the evening. Had supper at my folks' home where my darling had been since early in the afternoon. As usual, we enjoyed the stroll home.

## Saturday, Sept. 7

Got up about 10 a.m. We went to the Temple for awhile and then from there to the folks' where we had dinner. From there we strolled to Hermine's home and stayed there a short while. Hermine joined us for a stroll into the park, which we enjoyed a whole lot. We walked Hermine back to her home and then came home to our own little abode. After taking a bite, we went to Jersey City where we tried to obtain seats at the Majestic Theater; but without success. We also tried Keith's but there was a line about a block long waiting to get in, and even then there was standing room only. We walked thru the main business street for a while and then came home. But we were not as disappointed as one would expect. Our great love overcomes such little things and keeps us happy always.

## Sunday, September 8, 1918

Got up about nine, and my darling and I walked downtown where we separated. My wife went to the Synagogue where my mother was, and I went where my father was. After an hour or so I met my wife and went home. I invited Mr. E. Sobel to dinner and he walked home with us. Had a very nice dinner, after which we sat and conversed in the parlor until about five o'clock, when Mr. Sobel went home. After a little while, we went over to Pop Samuel's and stayed about an hour, after which we came home and sat in the parlor. We have been very happy these days—my darling and I. Each day we realize more and more how much we mean to each other, and greater and greater does my love for her become. It is New Year's today. *(Obviously this is the Jewish New Year, Rosh Hashanah.)* May her share this year be everything her dear heart desires.

*DAR*

## Tuesday, September 10, 1918

Took a nice little spin on wheel *(bicycle?)* after coming home from the office. After supper my sweetheart and I went over to visit Mr. and Mrs. Tessie Cohn. Enjoyable evening for us both. Played cards for a short while and then came home to bed at 10:30 P.M.

### Wednesday, Sept. 11, 1918

Came home from the office as usual, but while enjoying a nice supper received a message to report for work 'til midnight which I did. My darling was not feeling very well and I was somewhat worried most of the time. Home about midnight.

### Thursday, Sept. 12

A very happy day for us both. Came home from the office, at the usual time and after a most enjoyable supper my darling and I went to the movies and saw "The Hell with the Kaiser." It impressed us both very much. We are intensely happy tonight and feel that we are enjoying life upon this earth as it is given to few to enjoy. As for myself, I am living in the fullest sense of the word "live." My whole being is flooded and surges with supreme happiness and contentment. And all of which I owe to my dearest. It is a tremendous debt I owe her—may He who rules everything show me the way to repay her tenfold.

*Dave*

### Friday, September 13, 1918

Had a very enjoyable evening today. We went to the Opera House and saw quite a nice show. The movie played was "Tom Sawyer." Walked home and as usual we were in a very happy mood and felt that we had spent a nice day.

### Saturday, September 14, 1918

Today is my birthday and I am 22 years of age. My darling and I awoke at the same time and I had hardly opened my eyes when she placed her arms around me endearingly and congratulated me and wished me future happiness and longevity. It touched my heart deeply and almost brought tears to my eyes. Throughout my whole life there has never been anyone who ever paid any attention to a birthday of mine, and it must have been only natural that this expression of my darling's love for me should so move me.

My love also surprised me with something I had been longing for, for quite some time: a beautiful rubber plant which she had placed on the table where I would see it first thing in the morning. Attached to the plant she had placed a little note containing a few sacred little words of love and well wishing. Altho I worked from 7 a.m. to 7 p.m., which is quite a long day, I was in the best of spirits and very happy due to my darling's kindnesses and love.

In the evening she met me at the office and we called upon the cousins' family in the Bronx. After leaving them we walked thru the business streets for a while and then came home, reaching here about midnight. We had quite a nice evening of it, but towards the latter part my girlie began to feel bad and I was quite worried.

*(Mother probably didn't realize that she was pregnant with my sister, Emma Rothman Levin, who was born on May 25, 1919.)*

## Sunday, September 15, 1918

Another very happy day. We stayed in bed until about 10 o'clock. My wife and I played around like a couple of kids and enjoyed our home very much. I went in to the office about 1:30 p.m. and left there at 6:30 from where I went to my folks' for supper. Ruth was there too. We then went to the Synagogue for it was the evening before the "Day of Atonement," Yom Kippur. After services we walked home and as usual enjoyed it very much.

## Monday, September 16th 1918

Stayed in bed until 8 o'clock. Went to the Temple in the morning. It is "Yom Kippur" and we fasted all day. We walked around most of the day. In the afternoon we went to the city park and took a short nap on the grass. This was quite a novelty and we enjoyed it. Gee! But we were hungry. Honey pictured herself eating all kinds of good things. She stood the fast quite well but, poor darling, towards evening she became very sick to the stomach and of course it gave me a bad scare. She turned very white but thank God she came around in a short time and we were able to come home from the folks' where we had gone after she began to feel badly.

*(I wonder if Mother knew that she was pregnant. If so, she probably should not have been fasting. But they didn't have pregnancy tests in those days, and she was only one month into the pregnancy at that time.)*

## Tuesday, Sept 17, 1918

Passed a very quiet day. Stayed home in the evening. My wife read for a while and then knitted. After I took a warm bath we both retired. Sam *(David's brother)* and Mother Rothman were here.

## Wednesday, September 18, 1918

Honey didn't feel quite up to the mark, so we stayed home and went to bed early. Oh! I forgot, we went for a walk in the evening and intended going to the movies but they had a picture which we had already seen, so on the way home we stopped at Belle's *(brother Milton Samuel's wife)* and spent a pleasant evening there. To bed at 10 p.m.

## Thursday, September 19th

*(Mother writing):* I got up with Dave and after cleaning the house went to mother Rothman's to help her bake; but she had nothing ready so I sewed on the machine and made a bag. Left there at 3 p.m. and came right home. In the evening my darling and I took a walk and dropped in at the movies where we saw a most interesting and unusual picture, "The Whispering Chorus," which we enjoyed very much. To bed at 9:30 P.M.

## Friday, September 20th, 1918

*(Dad writing):* A happy day. As I was coming home from the office my darling surprised me by boarding the train I was on and riding with me to E. 22nd St from where we were going to the folks' for supper. On the way we stopped in at the jeweler's to have my darling's watch fixed and who should come walking in but my brother Morris. It was very surprising, as I had not seen him for about three months. We all had supper together. After supper, my darling and I came home and lounged around in the parlor. It is raining out and home feels good tonight. We have just finished eating some grapes. Honey is going to take a warm bath and then we will retire—.

## Saturday, September 21, 1918

For me it was a hard day. Worked from 7 a.m. until midnight. Honey brought my supper to the office and that is the most happy incident of the whole day for me.

## Sunday, September 22, 1918

My day off. Spent the day around town. Morris, Dora Brodman and another lady friend called in the afternoon. Enjoyable time. Spent most of the day walking around town and in the evening went to the Opera House in company with

Morris and D. Brodman. It was one year ago today that I kissed my future bride for the first time!

## Monday, September 23, 1918

Another quiet but happy day passed. Went to the movies with honey, and saw a good picture called "Desert Wooing." Gee, it is always the same, happy, happy, always happy.

## Tuesday, Sept 24, 1918

*(Mom writing:)* Took it easy all day and in the evening we felt so good we went to the Majestic Theatre in Jersey City and saw a Burlesque Show. It was called "The Burlesque Wonder Show." It was good and we enjoyed it very much but not as much as the last one we saw. To bed about midnight.

## Wednesday, September 25, 1918

An easy day again and I am still okay. Hope it keeps up for some time to come. In the evening we went over to my folks' and spent a pleasant time there. Mr. and Mrs. Cohen also came over. We left at 9 P.M. and went right to bed. It has been rather miserable all day but that does not dampen our happiness. May it always be so!!

## Thursday, September 26, 1918

*(Dad writing)* We are in good spirits today. After supper we went over to the folks (Samuel). Then Ruthie and I went to the bay and picked up a basket of wood which we brought home. Even in such a thing as this we find pleasure. After coming from the bay we sat in the parlor. I wrote letters while my darling knitted.

## Friday, September 27, 1918

Went to the folks' (Rothman's) for supper. Walked home, sat in the parlor, wrote letters, and then to bed. One day less to write about in this diary!

## Saturday, September 28th, 1918

*(Mother writing)*: I went to Mother Rothman's for dinner and then took a walk with her. Before dinner I went to Shul. At 3 o'clock, I went to the train and thence to meet Dave in Jersey City. We went up to visit Birdie Michaels and Floss was there too. Of course we had a pleasant evening but Dave didn't enjoy it

much, so he felt strange. We reached home at 10:15 P.M. and it felt good to be back again.

## Sunday, September 29th, 1918

Got up at 9 a.m. and lounged around until 1:30 when Dave went to work. I went to my folks' and then took a walk to the park with Ruth, Mother, and Jeanette Butte. In the evening I went down to the office and knitted until 10 o'clock when my sweetheart and I came home. Met Sissie and Flossie on train.

*What a small world this seems to be, with family visiting and meeting all over Bayonne!*

## Monday, Sep. 30th, 1918

*(Dad writing)*: Went down to the Bay and brought home some wood. Went down alone to my folks as Papa and Mama were both sick. Was quite worried. Lounged around the house a while and then turned in.

## Tuesday, October 1st 1918

Went over to the folks (Samuel's) with honey. Spent most of the evening there.

## Wednesday, October 2nd, 1918

Spent the evening at home. Honey knitted and I rested on the lounge. We are worried about each other as there is an epidemic of influenza in the country. Honey took a bath after which we went to bed.

## Thursday, October 3rd, 1918

*(Mom writing)*: Thank God! Both of us feel O.K. so far and hope it keeps up. In the early evening Hubby and I went to the bay for wood and enjoyed it very much. After supper we lounged around in the parlor a while and then took a short walk to Belle's. She was out and Milton was in bed, so we stayed a while and then came home and to bed.

## Friday, October 4th

*(Dad writing)*: Spent the whole evening around the house. I got out my winter suits and made them ready for use. Home felt good this particular night and I felt as contented as one could be. We retired at an early hour.

## Saturday, October 5, 1918

This was a hard day but it was enjoyed just the same. I worked until midnight and in the evening honey came down and stayed with me until it was time to go home. This makes my work so much easier and the time passes much quicker.

This day held a great deal of excitement for us. A series of terrific explosions occurred at Morgan, NJ and the very force of it shook our home to the very foundation; and we are over 20 miles away from where it occurred. One of the explosions awoke us in the middle of the night and we were quite shocked and frightened. The explosions continued most of the day. About 100 lives were lost and thousands made homeless. It was an ammunition plant that had gone up, and it was considered one of the greatest plants in the world.

## Sunday, October 6, 1918

This was a very happy day. It was my day off. We got out of bed about 9:30 a.m. and then started out to pay Herbert and Hattie *(Samuel—Mother's brother and sister-in-law)* a visit. We spent most of the day with them and enjoyed every minute of the time while with them. We took a walk through Farb Gourge (sic) which was quite interesting. I forgot to mention that we met Hermine *(Mother's oldest sister)* at Herb's.

In the evening on the way home we took a ride on a motor bus and enjoyed the sights very much. We passed through Morningside Park and Central Park. It was the first time I had passed through these places. I saw N.Y. University and Columbia College for the first time. I also saw Carnegie's and Vanderbilt's homes. Fifth Ave was wonderfully decorated with all kinds of flags on account of the Liberty Loan campaign. Search lights played on the passing crowds from many of the tall buildings. *(Don't forget that WW I was in progress during these days.)*

We got off the bus at about 42$^{nd}$ Street. The different stores had wonderful displays in the windows. It was exceedingly interesting to all of us. We saw model submarines, airships and battleships. There were all sorts of battle scenes, torpedoes, bullets, helmets, guns, gas masks, flame projectors, paintings and all sorts of novelties. All in all, this was a great big happy interesting day—this day which marked the beginning of our tenth month of married life.

## Monday, Oct. 7, 1918

Spent the evening home. Sat in the parlor and enjoyed ourselves in the usually happy way. Flossie came over also and spent the night with us.

## Tuesday, October 8, 1918

The influenza epidemic is still raging and we thank the Almighty that so far we are well. Spent the evening at home and enjoyed all the comforts that such a home as ours can give. Flossie came over for a while.

## Wednesday, October 9, 1918

Came home a few hours late today. Spent the evening at home and after taking a little walk, we went to bed. We cannot do very much these days on account of the Spanish Influenza Epidemic.

## Thursday, October 10, 1918

Came home late again. We are still both well and feel thankful. Went to bed early without going anywhere.

## Friday, October 11, 1918

Worked 'til late. Honey came to the office and waited for me. To bed about 10 P.M. Thank goodness we are still well.

Saturday, Oct 12
Sunday, Oct 13
Monday Oct 14
Tuesday Oct 15
Wednesday Oct 16
Thursday Oct 17
Friday Oct 18
Saturday Oct 19

*The above dates are bracketed and this was written on the right:*

These days have all been busy ones. Very little of interest has taken place. I worked late almost every day. Honey has not been feeling just right and has been in bed most of this time. Today is Saturday and thank God she feels much better. She has received a check of $10 from dear old "Cranky Aunt Regina" for tomorrow is her birthday. Even during such times as these, with war, plague, catastrophe, explosions and death everywhere, we can find it possible to be happy. Such is our love—the Lord be praised.

## Sunday, October 20, 1918

*(Mother writing):* Spent most of the day in bed but enjoyed the day anyhow. Hubby washed and had some time of it. It rained in the afternoon and was miserable. Flossie surprised me with a beautiful fern and in the evening she and Jeanette *(youngest sister)* came over and we all spent a very pleasant evening in the parlor. This ended my 20th birthday, the first birthday of my married life. I hope we will both live to enjoy many, many more.

## Monday, October 21, 1918

Felt much better today so got up at 10 a.m. and just cleaned around in the house all day. In the evening Mother and Pop Rothman and Sam came up and when they left we went to bed.

*I will omit some of the entries from here on, since they become rather repetitious.*

## Thursday, October 24th, 1918

Mother and Pop Rothman came up in the evening and when they left we went to bed. Ruth is getting worse. *(This must be another "Ruth." I don't know who this was.)*

## Friday, Oct. 25th, 1918

Morris came up in the evening and as we had not seen him in some time, we had a long chat. He left at 10 P.M. and we went to bed.

## Saturday, October 26th, 1918

Was over to Mother's all afternoon as Ruth is so very sick. Helped Mother and then came home. Poor Ruth's days are numbered. In the evening we took a short walk to Belle's and from there went to Mrs. Richards' as she had a piano for sale. We were not at all impressed with it so let it go. To bed at 7:30 P.M.

## Sunday, October 27th, 1918

Dave went to work at 1 P.M. this day and after dressing, I went to Mother's and helped her with poor Ruth. Mother cried in my arms and I guess she realized there is no hope for Ruth. In the evening went to Hermine's for supper and then came home and to bed.

### Monday, October 28, 1918

At last poor dear Ruth's sufferings are ended for she passed away at 5 P.M. May God bless her and let her rest peacefully until eternity.

I did very little today for I was anxiously awaiting news of Ruth and of course, felt dreadfully upset. They would not allow me to come over there. In the evening Dave went out with Pop to make different arrangements for the funeral etc. and we then retired early.

### Tuesday, October 29, 1918

Stayed home most of the day, and in the evening Pop Rothman came up for a little while. Floss stayed with us overnight. We all felt pretty blue.

### Wednesday, October 30th, 1918

Ruth was buried at 11 A.M. today and after the funeral Ma and Pa Rothman came over; also Minnie. She expected to see Ruth but came too late. In the afternoon Belle came over for me and I went over to the house to help cook something for the folks. Dave called up about 3:15 P.M. and told me to come to (???) to meet Ed Cohn as he had a piano for us to look at. Went up to Ed's house for supper and then dropped in for a moment at Herb's. Bought a piano and expect to have it tomorrow.

### Thursday, October 31st, 1918

*(Dad writing:)* This is a big day for honey dear, for her piano has arrived at last. Home has a new feeling about it now for the music sounds so strange and pleasant. Minnie came over for awhile in the evening. Ruthie dear played awhile and Minnie sang. I am so happy in my home now that I seldom care to go out—even to the theatre.

I feel out of sorts for the last few days—Guess it must be that my little darling is going away from me for awhile.

*(The piano was a lovely Knabe that stayed in my parents' home for many, many years. In the 1970's, they bought a Steinway baby grand, and gave the Knabe to me. I eventually traded it for a lovely Yamaha grand.)*
Here's a photo of Mother playing her new piano:

### Friday, November 1st, 1918

We stayed home all evening. I studied shorthand while my darling played the piano and sang. It was another of those wonderful, quiet happy evenings.

### Saturday, November 2nd, 1918

Went to Hermine's for supper and then we went to the Opera House where we enjoyed a very nice show. To bed about 10 P.M.

### Sunday, November 3, 1918

This day we spent very quietly. We spent most of the day at home.

In the evening Dave Samuel *(Mother's brother)* came home from Carup (sic). We went to Milton's for awhile. Had a little poker game there.

## Monday, November 4, 1918

*(Still Dad writing):* This was a quiet day. Father came over in the evening. Sammy came later and Ruth dear played the piano for a little while. After taking a little stroll we went to bed.

## Tuesday, November 5, 1918

This is Election Day. I came home from the office a few hours earlier than usual. Honey and I took a little walk in the afternoon, and in the evening we stayed home.

## Wednesday, November 6, 1918

Today I feel mighty out of sorts and gloomy for my darling is going away for a few weeks. I escorted her to Penn Station and as I kissed her goodbye, I felt very blue indeed. I hope with all my heart and soul that she has a good rest.

*(Mother was going to Southold to visit her Aunt Regina, my "Nana." Nana was really my great-aunt; but she seemed like my grandmother. My real grandmother, Nana's half-sister Emma, had died when my mother was 12.)*

## Thursday, November 7, 1918

This is the first day that my darling is away from me and I feel blue indeed. Had supper at Ruth's home. Early to bed.

## Friday, November 8

Received two letters from honey which cheered me up a bit. Had supper with folks. Morris was home. Took a little walk with him. Went to the Opera and saw fairly good show. Morris stayed with me overnight.

## Saturday, November 9, 1918

Spent part of the night with my darling's folks and also part of it with a few friends. Went to bed at 8 P.M. I felt terribly lonely without my girlie. I went to sleep so early because I realized sleep was the only thing to let me forget my loneliness.

**Sunday, November 10.**

All day I feel alone and blue. A few friends came over to play cards. We had a very exciting game. Came home from work at 11 P.M.

# 9

## *Armistice Day*

### Monday, November 11, 1918

(*Dad writing:*) Today is a wonderfully joyous day for at last, after many months of suffering and suspense for both my darling and myself, a peace armistice has been signed. My pen is incapable of expressing what this means to this suffering, war-torn world. What mothers will be cheered, what hearts gladdened, and what monstrous crimes and injustices will be put an end to! As to myself, I feel like a slave freed from the yoke of slavery. Oh, what would I not have given to have had my sweetheart with me on this glorious day. We were given a half holiday at the office and when I got home and was alone, I had quite some difficulty in restraining myself from weeping with joy so greatly did it affect me.

Sirens shrieked, whistles blew and bells rang all day long while the streets were thronged with people. After having supper with Milton, he and I went to New York to celebrate the event. Never before in my life have I seen so joyous and so big a crowd of people in the streets. Some avenues were simply choked up with masses of people and to pass through was an impossibility. We followed the crowds for a few hours and then went to Proctor's 4th Avenue Theatre where we saw a very good show. We got home at an early hour of the morning.

### Tuesday, November 12, 1918

I feel much happier and lighthearted today as the time is drawing near when I shall be on my way to my darling. I met Herb after I was through at the office and went with him for a suit but could get none. To bed early.

### Wednesday, November 13, 1918

Spent most of the evening getting ready to leave tomorrow. I am dreadfully impatient. Took a nice bath and went early to bed.

## Thursday, November 14, 1918

At last the time has come, and I am on my way to my dear wife. I am writing this on the train and I just can't wait until I reach my own darling in Southold. This train would not be moving too fast for me if it were moving at 500 miles an hour.

## Friday, November 15, 1918

*(Mother writing):* Was so glad to be with my darling again, especially as I had been feeling so miserable. In the afternoon we went to the village and had ice cream and candy and on the way home we stopped to pick apples and enjoyed it immensely. In the evening we went to bed early.

## Saturday, November 16th, 1918

We arose at about 10 A.M. and after having breakfast went into the garden and picked beets, carrots etc. to send home. In the afternoon I went to the foot of the lane to watch the parade they had in honor of the peace—and it was all very well gotten up. In the evening honey and I walked to the village and Aunt Regina went in the car. They had a short but very interesting peace celebration, there being two very good speakers so we enjoyed it all very much.

## Sunday, November 17th, 1918

Were busy all morning getting ready to leave and Aunt Regina left with us. We took the afternoon train and enjoyed the trip a great deal, as there was a military band of 28 pieces which had been in Southold for the celebration and went to Camp Upton on our train. They played all the way to their station. We reached home at 8:45 P.M. very tired but I was glad to be home again.

## Monday, November 18th, 1918

Back to the old life again and as the place was none too clean, both Aunt Regina and I dug in good and hard so we were glad to go to bed early. Went to Mother's for a little while in the afternoon.

## Tuesday, November 19th, 1918

Aunt Regina went to NY with Pa and after finishing up the remaining cleaning that was to be done, I went to Mother's for dinner. Aunt Regina came back at 2 P.M. and after sitting around awhile, we went home and enjoyed the evening in the parlor.

## Wednesday, November 20th, 1918

We went to NY with Aunt Regina to shop and came home at 5 P.M. Sammy was up for supper and Pop Rothman came in the evening. We spent the evening home.

## Thursday, November 21st, 1918

This was some busy day. Had the washwoman in the morning and in the evening I entertained Flossie's knitting club and everyone enjoyed themselves. They left at 10:30 P.M. and we retired.

## Friday, November 22nd, 1918

Rested almost all day as I was so tired out. Aunt Regina left about 9:30 A.M. to spend a few days at Hasberg's. Went to Mother's for dinner and in the evening stayed home and went to bed early.

## Saturday, November 23rd. 1918

Had dinner at Mother's and after dinner Mother and I walked down to my mother-in-law where we visited a short while. Came home and after supper honey and I went to the Majestic Theatre in Jersey City and saw a pretty good show—but not so good as the first we saw some time ago.

*(After my grandmother, Emma Noé Samuel died, my grandfather, Joseph Samuel married Lina. I'm sure that it is Lina whom my mother calls "Mother" in this diary.)*

## Sunday, November 24th, 1918

Had a busy day as I finished the ironing. Aunt Regina came home at 5:45 P.M. and I was glad to see her again. Mrs. Hasberg sent a lovely vase for the table. Honey worked until 10 P.M. and I sat up until he came as Lillian Thomas was here waiting for her folks.

Went to Mother's in the afternoon and spent the evening in the parlor with honey while Aunt Regina and Flossie went to visit Hermine. To bed at 9 P.M.

## Tuesday, November 26th, 1918

Had Mrs. Dorn and Mother up for afternoon tea and spent a very pleasant time. They left about 5 P.M. and we stayed home in the evening as I didn't feel very well. To bed early.

### Wed., November 27th, 1918

Aunt Regina and Floss left for Atlantic City and I went to the train with them. From there went to Belle's and then came home, had supper and went to bed early as my darling worked until midnight.

### Thursday, November 28th, 1918

'Tis Thanksgiving Day and we have lots of things to be grateful for indeed, so to celebrate the day we were invited to Hermine's for a big Thanksgiving dinner. The whole family was there and we all had a very nice time. Came home at 7 P.M. and went to bed at 9 P.M.

### Friday, November 29, 1918

Went to the folks for a short visit and then we all went to Belle's as Rhoda was not well. Stayed a little while and then came to our own little nest and to bed.

*(Rhoda Samuel was the baby daughter of Belle and Milton Samuel, mother's sister-in-law and brother.)*

### Saturday, November 30, 1918

Went to the Lyceum for the first time and saw a nice show and enjoyed the music very much. Came home at 9:30 P.M. and went to bed.

### Sunday, December 1st, 1918

We arose at 10 A.M. and after preparing dinner took the 1:30 train to NY and we just enjoyed ourselves on the East Side, watching the quaint people with all their pushcarts and good things to eat. I brought home bread and a lot of other good things which we feasted with when we came home at 5:30 P.M. Aunt Regina got back from Atlantic city at 10 P.M. and after she had told us all the news we went to sleep.

### Monday, December 2nd, 1918

Had a quiet day and in the evening went to the Lyceum where we saw a very interesting picture, "America's Answer," which was on the style of Pathé News. From there we went to the folks for a short stay and then came home and to bed.

## Tuesday, December 3rd, 1918

Aunt Regina went home today. We left Bayonne at 8:30 A.M., Aunt Regina intending to get the 10 A.M. train but when we got to the station found that it left at 9:19 so we just bummed around in the various stores all day and at 3:30 P.M. I left Aunt R. at the Penn Station and met Dave at the Jersey Central Railroad where we both went to the dentist. From there we went to Mother Rothman's and had supper and then came home dead tired.

## Wednesday, December 4th, 1918

Mama died eight years ago today, and I forgot to burn a candle for her. Spent a very quiet day as I didn't feel well after all of yesterday's bumming. Went to bed early.

## Thursday, December 5th, 1918

I washed as Mrs. Daly didn't show up. Felt all in afterwards so didn't go to Sophie A.'s in the evening. Went to bed early.

## Friday, December 6, 1918

Went to Mother R's for supper and enjoyed it very much. After supper we went to the Opera House and saw a very good show. All Bayonne was there so we were lucky to get a seat way up in the balcony. Saw Charlie Chaplin in "Shoulder Arms." After the show we had something to drink and then walked home.

## Saturday, December 7th, 1918

Had a very pleasant day as we went to East New York to visit Eva *(and Tommy Atkins, the cousins who had the flower shop)* and they received us royally. We enjoyed ourselves very much and reached home at 12:30 A.M. feeling fine.

## Sunday, December 8th, 1918

Got up at 10:45 A.M. and after I prepared dinner, honey left on the 1:35 P.M. train for work and I took it easy. In the evening Hermine, Jake and Emeline came for supper and they left at 9:30 P.M. *(Hermine was Mother's oldest sister; Jake [Jacob Levin] her husband, and Emeline their daughter.)*

## Monday, December 9th, 1918

In the afternoon went downtown for a chicken and in the evening just sat in the parlor and enjoyed home. To bed early.

## Tuesday, December 10th, 1918

Met Honey at the dentist where he finished my tooth. We went home, had supper and sat in parlor until bed time.

## Wednesday, December 11th, 1918

Went over to my folks to spend the evening as we hadn't been there for such a long time. Left at about 8:30 P.M. and went home and to bed.

## Thursday, December 12th, 1918

Was supposed to go to see "Heart of the World" with mother in the afternoon but she went to NY instead, so in the evening honey and I went to see it and enjoyed it very much. Met Milt and Jeanette there. Reached home at 11 P.M. and retired.

*This diary is getting rather long, but it includes the highlights of the life of David and Ruth Samuel Rothman. It was interesting to me to know how close the family was, and how they were constantly visiting each other and sharing meals.*

*Also amazing were the long hours that Dad worked. Usually he worked for 9 hours at a stretch. Unions were certainly needed! Apparently, Dad did earn high pay for his work, in the climate of those times.*

*These were the days of hand-washing the clothes and extensive ironing. None of today's conveniences were available. At least the piano wasn't too different from today's instruments!*

## Thursday, December 19, 1918

Pop Rothman was here in the evening and waited for Dave to come home, as Dave went to the Dentist first. Dave came at 6:30 P.M. and Pa left. We had supper and then went to the Lyceum to see "Les Miserables" which we enjoyed very much. Met Sam at the theatre. To bed at 9:30 P.M.

## Saturday, December 21st, 1918

This is the shortest day of winter and so far we have had wonderful weather. Before we know it summer will be here again and with it I hope will come our little darling. Goodness! How long it seems to wait. Heard that Aunt Betsy is very sick and is expected to die any day. Honey worked until 8:30 P.M. today and until he came home I enjoyed our little nest thoroughly and spent the time sewing and just doing as I pleased. What more can one want in life? My only wish is that our lot will never be worse than it is today! To bed at 10 P.M.

### Tuesday, December 25, 1918

'Tis Christmas Day and a lovely sunny one, too. Honey went to work at 8 A.M. and came home at 12:30 P.M. and we went to Mother's for a delicious dinner. Herb and Hattie *(Ruth's brother and his wife)*, Floss and Jeanette were here for supper and they left about 7 P.M. Dave *(Ruth's brother David Samuel)* stayed overnight. Honey came home about 9:15 P.M. and we retired.

### Friday, December 27th, 1918

Went to Mother Rothman's for our usual Friday (Sabbath) supper and walked home, enjoying the stores on our way. Dave *(brother)* slept overnight. Retired 9:30 P.M.

### Sunday, December 29th, 1918

*(Still Mother speaking:)* Morris *(Dad's brother)* was here for dinner and he left with honey at 1:30 P.M. for work. Minnie came up with a friend and we all walked to Bertha's where we spent a very enjoyable afternoon. We left at 5:45 P.M. after having refreshments and I came to our little nest where I am now writing up "our diary." It is 6:30 P.M. and I miss my darling so much but must "grin and bear it" until better times come. Am going to play the piano now.

### Monday, December 30th, 1918

Met Dave at the office at 4 P.M. and we then went to the stores to do a little shopping and then went to the Pennsylvania Station to meet Aunt Regina. From there we went to Rigs and had supper and then came home and soon retired. I was sure glad to have dear Auntie with me again.

### Tuesday, December 31st, 1918

I washed and Aunt R. went to NY to visit the Hasbergs. In the afternoon. Moe Wolf and Irv came for a short visit. After supper the folks all came over and we had a lovely evening. To bed about 10:30 P.M. and woke up at midnight in time to hear them ringing in the New Year.

## Wednesday, January 1st, 1919

'Tis the first day of the New Year and although it is not very pleasant weather we are happy as usual. We bustled all morning and Floss came for dinner, after which we got the 12:20P.M. train for N.Y. and met hubby at the theater where we went to see "The Mikado." We enjoyed it immensely and after the performance came to our nest and enjoyed the evening in the parlor. To bed early.

## Thursday, January 2nd, 1919

It rained all day so we stayed home and enjoyed the whole day in the parlor. To bed early.

## Friday, January 3rd, 1919

Went to New York about 10:30 A.M. with Aunt Regina and went to Miss Rothchild's for dinner, where we sure had some dinner! Left there at about 4:30 P.M. and met Honey at Herb's where we had supper and then met Aunt Regina at the 116th Street subway station where we all went to the Pennsylvania Station to see Aunt Regina off for the balmy South and we were sorry to see her go. *(I think that Nana spent winters in Miami, Florida. Mother, Bobby and I joined her in 1936, after I had been ill. Dad joined us for a week, and then we took a ship, the* Shawnee, *back to New York.)*

We left at 8:45 P.M. and home surely felt good after such a long but pleasant day.

## Saturday, January 4th, 1919

Not much happened on this day, as honey worked until midnight and I took it easy all day.

## Sunday, January 5th, 1919

Honey went to work at 8 A.M. and came home at 4:30 P.M. Mother Rothman and Morris were here in the evening. Mother left at 8:20 P.M. and Morris stayed overnight. To bed early.

## Monday, January 6th, 1919

We are married one year today, and as I look back on that year, it is all like a wonderful dream which seems to be but a day old; and then again as though it were never any different. So far, in this one year, I should call ours a successful adventure for not only have all my fond dreams come true but the reality has far surpassed my dearest dream and for this I am so happy. I am almost afraid such happiness cannot last long and hope God will always be so good to us in the years to come.

In the evening Honey and I went to the Lyceum and saw "Mickey" which we enjoyed very much. To bed 10 P.M.

## Tuesday, January 7th, 1919

Honey worked until midnight again and I went to Pop's for supper. In the evening Floss and I paid Minnie a little visit and I came home about 10 P.M. In the meantime Pop Rothman had brought me a kitten, which he left at Miss T's for me and now we have a new institution in our household which honey has named "Nickey."

## Wednesday, January 8th, 1919

Minnie came over in the afternoon for a little while and then honey came home at 3:30 P.M. and we took a nice walk and did the marketing. In the evening Jeanette, Floss and Pearl Cooper came up and we had a very pleasant time together until 10 P.M. when they left and we retired.

## Thursday, January 9th, 1919

Honey worked until midnight and I went to Pop's for supper, and in the evening the Thursday Evening Club met at the house so we had a very pleasant time. To bed at 11 P.M.

## Friday, January 10th, 1919

Went to Honey's folks for the usual Friday night meal and enjoyed it very much. Stopped in for the table on the way home and found it fixed beautifully. To bed early.

## Saturday, January 11th, 1919

Honey worked until midnight again so I went to the folks' for dinner and in the afternoon took a walk with them to Hermine's as she had been sick. Reached home about 6 P.M. and worked on Midgey's bag.

## Sunday, January 12th, 1919

This is the first Sunday Honey was off in three weeks, so we enjoyed it by staying in our nest and in the afternoon went to see "Intolerance" which we enjoyed very much. To bed early.

## Monday, January 13th, 1919

Honey worked until midnight again so I had dinner at the folks' but came home early and spent the time in the house. To bed early.

## Tuesday, January 14th, 1919

Honey worked until 5:20 P.M. and in the evening Floss and Jeanette came over. We sat in the parlor and they left about 9:45 P.M. We then retired.

## Wednesday, January 15th, 1919

We did not get up until 8:15 A.M. as Honey's hours have been changed to 10:30 A.M. until 6:45 P.M. and I think we will like this much better. It was a beautiful day so I busied myself around the house and in the afternoon took a walk to Rothman's. Pa R. came back with me and stayed until Dave came home. In the evening we went to the folks to say good-bye as they sail for Florida tomorrow. Came home at 9 P.M. and wrote to Aunt Regina for her birthday and we then retired.

## Thursday, January 16th, 1919

The folks left for Florida and Floss came here to live with us. We stayed home in the evening and retired early while Floss went to Belle's to the club.

## Friday, January 17th, 1919

Spent a quiet day as I washed, and in the evening sat in the parlor and as usual enjoyed it more than a show. To bed at 10 P.M.

## Saturday, January 18th, 1919

Was supposed to go to N.Y. with Floss but the weather was too uncertain; so in the afternoon went down to the folks on 22nd Street and had Pop go to the East Side with Dave and me, where Honey bought a nice overcoat. Went to see Dave's folks over there and reached home at about 2:30 P.M. After having a fresh hot bread sandwich we retired.

### Sunday, January 19th, 1919

Arose about 9 A.M. and after having dinner we took a walk to Cooper's where we had a very enjoyable visit and then took a walk with Pearl, Harry and Sam to 22nd Street and back. Spent the evening in the parlor. To bed early.

### Monday, January 20th, 1919

Aunt Regina's 56th birthday and I missed being with her this day but was thinking of her all the time. I didn't feel real well so took it easy. Honey went from work to get a suit and came home about 9:15 P.M. We then retired.

# 10

## *The Flu Epidemic of 1918*

### Tuesday, January 21st, 1919

Belle *(Meyerwicz Samuel, Milton's wife, and mother of baby Rhoda)* got sick with the flu so we were anxious about her. In the evening Floss went to see her and we went to the movies and saw "An Eye for an Eye" which we enjoyed very much.

### Wednesday, January 22nd, 1919

Morris came up and we all went over to Appel's where we spent a very pleasant evening and came home about 11 P.M. and retired.

### Thursday, January 23rd, 1919

It rained very hard but Floss went to the meeting at Bessie Goldman's and we spent an enjoyable evening in the parlor. To bed early.

### Friday, January 24th, 1919

Had word that they took Belle to Swiney's sanitarium as she had gotten worse and Milt took sick at Belle's folks' house. We are worried of course. In the evening Morris came up and we sang until bed time.

### Saturday, January 25th, 1919

Went to N.Y. with Honey on the 10 A.M. train and after shopping for baby's things at Hearn's, met Floss at Macy's and then had a Chop Suey dinner which we both enjoyed very much. Went back to Macy's, and after bumming around came home about 6:30 P.M. and spent the evening in the parlor. To bed early.

### Sunday, January 26th, 1919

Honey worked from 8 A.M. to 4 P.M. and I spent a quiet day as I didn't feel well. In the evening we just enjoyed home until bedtime, which was quite early.

### Monday, January 27th, 1919

Honey worked from 7 A.M. to 3 P.M. and after having our supper we went to N.Y. and first went to Dr. Weisman's where Dave was examined in order to join the Lodge. We then went to the Park Theatre where we saw Alice Brady in "Forever After" and enjoyed it immensely. Reached home at 12:45 P.M. after a pleasant time.

### Tuesday, January 28th, 1919

Went over to Sophie's in the afternoon and found her sick. Stayed a little while and then came home and sewed. In the evening Morris came up and we sang. He left at 10 P.M. and we retired.

### Wednesday, January 29th, 1919

In the evening, Floss went down to see Milton and we stayed home. Belle is in very critical condition and Milton is not at all well. We retired early.

### Thursday, January 30th, 1919

In the evening Honey and I went to Tessie's to see Hermine in reference to Belle. Stayed a little while and then came home. Floss was home from work all day as she didn't feel well. Morris came up in the evening and we sang a little while and then retired.

### Friday, January 31st, 1919

In the evening went to Dave's folks where we enjoyed the usual Friday night supper and then came home. Floss went to see Milton and found Belle very sick. To bed early.

### Saturday, Feb. 1st, 1919

Belle just the same, with only a fighting chance.—Entertained Morris and Lillian Adler for supper and spent a very pleasant evening. They left at 10:30 P.M. and we retired.

## Sunday, February 2nd, 1919

Arose about 9 A.M. and after taking it easy and having dinner we went to N.Y. to visit Hattie and had supper. I left about 9 P.M. and Honey and Herb went to the Kempner's Lodge. Herb and Moe were in Bayonne to see Milt and found Belle in a very critical condition with only a fighting chance. Poor Milt looks terrible. I reached home about 10:30 P.M. and Honey came home about 2 A. M.

## Monday, February 3rd, 1919

Belle is very much worse and there is no hope. We all feel very blue and can't do anything to help. We stayed home in the evening and went to bed early as honey works from 7–3 tomorrow.

## Tuesday, Feb. 4th, 1919

Poor Belle died at 3 A.M. and we all felt dreadful. Floss didn't go to work and when honey came home he went down to cheer up Milt a bit. Herb and Moe were also there but poor Milt is pretty hard hit. Honey came home at 7 P.M. And after sitting in the parlor a while we retired.

## Wednesday, Feb. 5th, 1919

Dave didn't work today as he went to Belle's funeral. In the afternoon Florence was up with Rhoda and in the evening after going to see Milton we went to the Lyceum to get things off our mind a while. To bed at 10 P.M.

*Milton Samuel was Mother's brother, and his wife Belle died in the flu epidemic of 1918–19. They had a baby at the time, Rhoda. Milton eventually married Florence (Florrie) Cooper, and they had two more children, Eleanore and Rosalind. The family moved to Mattituck, Long Island, and they operated a clothing store there. They lived behind (and later above) the store. We were close to those relatives and spent many Sundays with them. Milton was the fine violinist who later played at the Einstein evenings, with the quartets. It was he who introduced me to accompanying and chamber music at the piano. I sight read all the great violin Concerti and Sonatas with him from the age of eight years.*

## Thursday, Feb 6th, 1919

Went to Hermine's in the afternoon and took Rhoda out for a walk. Met Honey at Milt's at 4 P.M. and came home for supper. Spent the evening in the parlor and Morris was up for a short time.

## Friday, February 7th, 1919

Went to Honey's folks' for supper and then visited Milt for a short time. Reached home about 9 P.M. and after sitting in the parlor a while, went to bed.

## Saturday, February 8th, 1919

*(This is my Dad writing:)* This day held a great surprise in store for me. The nature of this surprise is in fact the reason for my resuming the narration of the very many pleasant events that occur in the course of a happy existence. One day about three months ago I suddenly decided for certain reasons to discontinue the writing of these incidents. And all this time I had been under the impression that this dear diary was a thing of the past—just laid aside and forgotten. But many a time have I been sorry—sorry beyond expression, for often have I thought that it would certainly be a shameful thing to let the many pleasant happenings of our happy life go by unrecorded and probably forgotten. So imagine my surprise, my wonderful and inexpressible pleasure, when, by mere chance, I opened this diary, simply to glance over what I had written in the past, which seems so far away, imagine—to find that my dear, darling wife, my wonderful wife, had picked up this diary which I had thrown aside, and resumed for three whole months the narration of the long remembered events of all this time. And to think that I had not known a blessed thing about it! It was indeed a pleasure, this surprise, but it moved me, too.

This evening Miss Pearl Cooper surprised us with a visit. As usual we had a very pleasant evening.

## Sunday, February 9th, 1919

Was off this day and my darling and I enjoyed it immensely. We took a walk in the afternoon after having a short nap. In the evening Herb and Hattie and Mr. and Mrs. Appel were here and stayed for supper. Afterwards we went over to Appel's home and listened to some good records on the victrola.

## Monday, February 10th, 1919

*(Mother, Ruth Rothman writing:)* Spent the evening home and enjoyed it as usual. To bed at 10:45 P.M.

## Tuesday, Feb. 11th, 1919

Went to Hermine's in the afternoon and took a walk to Mother Rothman's where we had tea. Spent the evening sewing and writing. To bed at 10 P.M.

## Wednesday, Feb. 12th, 1919

*(Dad writing:)* I was off for the day, Lincoln's Birthday. My darling and I went to the city where we had a chop suey dinner. This was my first attempt at Chinese dishes. I think it's the last, too. After dinner we went to the Park Theatre where we saw an opera called "Robin Hood." We enjoyed it immensely for the music was very good. In the evening we stayed at home and when it was time to go to bed we both felt that we had spent a very happy day.

## Sunday, Feb. 16th, 1919

*(Mother writing:)* Honey worked the 5 to 12 trick so after having a good dinner we walked a short distance and after honey left I sewed and played the piano until bed time.

## Monday, Feb. 17th, 1919

Didn't wash as I felt all in for some reason or other, so took it easy all day and in the evening, after enjoying ourselves thoroughly at Mrs. Appel's as Honey played the Robin Hood record, we came home and retired. It is surely wonderful to be contented with all the ordinary-day things and just enjoy having each other. May it always be so.

## Wednesday, Feb. 19th, 1919

*(Dad writing):* Milton came up again in the evening and after having a nice long talk we turned in, Milton staying with us overnight.

## Thursday, Feb. 20th, 1919

Milton came up again in the evening and we had another nice chat. He stayed overnight. Our home looks nicer to us all the time. Never seem to tire of it. Don't mind staying in night after night

### Saturday, Feb. 22, 1919

*(Dad speaking):* This is Washington's Birthday and I came home from the office early. I got into different clothes and took honey to the Lyceum where we spent the evening.

### Sunday, Feb. 23rd, 1919

*(Mother writing):* In the afternoon we started out for a walk, first stopping at Appel's but found them out so wended our way downtown. We stopped to visit Tessie's, as Eddie and Mae were visiting them, and they made us stay for supper. We enjoyed the day very much and got home at about 9:15 P.M. and retired. Had a telegram from Buster stating that he had arrived safely in New York. *(Buster is Charles Rothman, Dad's brother. Buster fought in World War I and was one of the oldest soldiers in World War II. We had some letters from him that described his war experiences.)*

### Monday, Feb. 24th, 1919

In the afternoon Sophie and Tessie called for me and we went for a walk which I enjoyed very much as the weather was ideal. Met Hermine on the way and had a chat with her. In the evening we sat in the parlor and then retired early.

### Tuesday, Feb. 25th, 1919

Pearl Cooper surprised us with a visit in the evening and Morris was also here. We played the piano and sang until 9:30 P.M. I served ice cream which we all enjoyed. We retired at 11 P.M. after a lovely evening. Aunt Regina is coming home. Hurrah!

### Wednesday, Feb. 26th, 1919

This day I spent in the city bumming and buying all the various things I needed. Came home on the 6:20 P.M. train with honey and we went directly to Mother Rothman's for supper. Reached home dead tired at 9 P.M. and went to bed.

*This was the last entry for 1919. On May 25, 1919, my sister, Emma Leah Rothman (Levin) was born ... the first child of David and Ruth Samuel Rothman. As related in the biography section of my Dad, Mother and Dad had decided that they didn't want to raise children in the paved city streets of Bayonne or New York. Therefore, Dad gave up his lucrative (as it was then considered) job with the Jersey Central Railroad and they moved to Southold.*

*They sold the house that Grandpa Joseph Samuel had given them, and used the proceeds from that sale to buy a building in the tiny town of Southold, on the North Fork of Long Island. It seemed like the end of the world, in those days. It was about a 100 mile drive on poor roads. However, the train also ran from Pennsylvania Station to Southold. The railroad station was quite close to the store. We could hear the steam engines from the house.*

*Mother's Aunt Regina had a home in Southold, and Mother and Jeanette used to visit Aunt Regina regularly from the time that they were quite young. It was the only place in the country that Mother was familiar with, so that's where Mom and Dad bought property. Dad opened Rothman's Department Store, the store where he met Albert Einstein. As it was explained, Dad sold appliances, clothing, and whatever was in demand at any particular time. He reasoned that if he didn't spend more than he earned, he would not go "broke."*

*More entries in the diary:*

## September 28th, 1921

Our second child, Arthur Ozias Rothman, was born in Greenport hospital. Dr. Stevens delivered him and had to use instruments. I was quite torn and felt pretty miserable until the stitches were taken out on the 8th day. We had the Bris in the hospital and Pop Rothman was there. Went home the 11th day—pretty weak too but am nursing this time.

*(In those days, new mothers were kept in bed for a long time, unlike today when new mothers resume normal activities as soon as possible.*

*I guess that with all the child care needed, Mother and Dad had no time to write in the diary.)*

## March 24, 1922

Received word this morning that our dear sister Flossie passed away in childbirth, and my heart is overflowing for that dear little motherless girl that she left behind and for Abe (Ravitz) who is heartbroken. 'Tis the first of the breakup of our family and I hope the lapse will be many, many years before more sorrow comes to us. God bless little Jeanne and keep her from harm. She was born last Friday.

*Jeanne was re-named "Flossie" after her deceased mother. Flossie used to visit us in Southold quite often. It was she who taught me to read books for amusement. We went to the library together and checked out books. After that, I was an avid reader.*

*On June 28, 1927, Robert Herman Rothman, my brother, was born.*

*In March, 1928, Arthur Ozias (Buddy) Rothman died of peritonitis from a burst appendix. This was such a tragic loss for Mother and Dad that they never recovered from the grief.*

*On May 3, 1930, I (Joan Regina Rothman Brill Kallmeyer) was born.*

*To help with his sadness over Buddy, Dad decided to learn to play the violin. When I was small, I used to hear Mother and Dad playing together at the piano and violin. It made a great impression on me, as I learned to play the piano from the age of 3. Uncle Morris Rothman was helping Dad in the store; and one day he taught me to play "Mary Had A Little Lamb" on the piano. Then he taught me "Twinkle, Twinkle Little Star." Then he taught me how to add chords; and from then on, I played everything I heard by ear. I started lessons at about 4 years, and when I was 5, my sister took me to school with her to play the piano for the first grade students. (There was no kindergarten in those days.) I still remember the songs that I played on that occasion!*

*It was in 1939 that Mother became ill with the flu, or some other undiagnosed illness, as described earlier in this book. During that same summer, Albert Einstein was a visitor to Nassau Point, and the friendship between Einstein and my father became a reality.*

*I will now continue with Dad's Einstein story, and will continue the diary at the end of this book.*

# 11

## *Some Signs of the Times*

*What was happening in the world in 1939? Hitler was in the middle of his march to rule the world.*

*My father was a GE dealer at Rothman's Department Store, one of the earliest dealers in New York State. Their motto at the time was: "Be a GE Dealer and See the World." If you sold enough appliances, you could qualify for free trips and cruises.*

*Well, Dad sold enough appliances to earn a cruise to Havana, Nassau and Miami on the Polish vessel, the* MS Pilsudsi. *This time, the entire family took the cruise ... Dad, Mother, my sister Emma, my brother Bob, and I. Here is what I remember:*

*In March, 1939, I was almost 9 years old. We visited Havana, Nassau and Miami. The weather was beautiful. I remember that there was a dance one night. Emma was all dressed up in a blue strapless gown, and she met a young man whom she liked quite a bit. He kept in touch after the cruise, and visited her in Southold. Em saw him a few years ago ... just bumped into him by accident! Small world.*

*Some days we sat in the deck chairs, and the Deck Steward would come around with tea and baked potatoes and other goodies. We got to know him quite well ... I don't remember his name.*

*I remember that the ship stopped in Havana. The dictator Fulgencio Batista was the ruler at the time. Everything was very orderly and beautiful. There were flowers everywhere. However, there were also beggars everywhere we went, begging and pleading for money. If you gave anyone a nickel, all the beggars would follow you unmercifully. It was so sad. They looked sick and hungry.*

*One of the activities planned aboard ship was an amateur contest. (They still have the same routine on cruises today!) Anyway, a rehearsal was scheduled, but the sea was so rough that day that everyone was seasick; so the rehearsal was canceled. I assumed that the show was canceled, too. I also was seasick.*

*Later in the day, the sea became calmer, and the show was to go on. Although I was just 8 ¾ years old at the time, I still remember the day clearly, for it would mark one of my first public performances.*

*I was the first performer. I played Beethoven's Sonata in G Major, Op. 49 No. 1. I rattled through it. There was an upright piano, and I think there was a microphone, but the wind blew so hard I could hardly hear myself. The show was held up on deck.*

*I finished the first half, and everyone started to applaud. I wanted to play the rest, but they stopped me. I guess they thought I had played long enough! Anyway, at the end, they declared that I had won the contest, and presented me with a beautiful polish doll, all dressed in a red, traditional costume. Of course, I was thrilled! I have treasured that doll all of my life.*

*Dad got a beautiful big poster of the ship, and he put it in his office. It is still there today, 26 years after Dad's death. We all remembered that cruise with wonder and affection.*

*On September 1ˢᵗ, 1939, Germany declared war on Poland, and the MS Pilsudski became a troop carrier. Imagine our distress when we learned that shortly thereafter, the ship hit a mine and had sunk. The entire crew, including the deck steward, had perished with the ship.*

# 12

## *Beliefs and Miscellany*

*Some time later, Dad did continue his narration. Here are more of his memories of that historic summer:*

You know, Joan, I am often asked about his religious beliefs. Well, one evening during an intermission of the quartette playing, we walked outside together into the garden. It was a warm, beautiful night, the moon was full and we began talking about the beauties of nature and how wonderful it was to contemplate the movement of the planets, the sun, the stars and the moon and the heavens; what a beautiful arrangement it all was and suddenly I asked him,

"And what are your feelings about religion?"

And he replied something like this: "You can be sure that I do not believe in an anthropomorphic God. You understand what I mean by anthropomorphic ..."

And I told him I did.

"However, after many years of contemplation and observation of the beauty and mathematical preciseness of the natural laws that obtain in the universe, I am amazed and awed with wonder. And before all this, I have a great feeling of deep humbleness. And that is my religion. There must have been a guiding superior intelligence to have achieved such perfection.

"I have no use for organized religion and feel that mankind would be better off without it."

That was it, Joan. And as you know, that's just about the way it is with me.

Here are some other thoughts from the auto trip to inspect the RCA plant in Riverhead, an item that offers some indication of Einstein's modesty:

Einstein's words: "I haff always been astonished at the great fuss and publicity and fame that has come to me over my special work, which so few are supposed to understand. After all, I have only interpreted and drawn conclusions from the work of others: Max Plank, Maxwell Lawrence, Monk, Fitzgerald, Poincare, Michelson and Morley and others."

On another occasion, he was trying to explain something to me in the field of relativity. And he was getting over my head and so I told him laughingly, "Look, after all, I've only had an eighth grade schooling and I know nothing about mathematics; and therefore you will have very little success in trying to explain this to me. After all, an eighth-grader!"

And he laughed and said, "Upon the other hand, when someone tells me he has had a college education, I am somewhat suspicious!"

I think he meant by this that he had no respect for a college man unless he was able to *think*, and didn't take much truck in the fact that one had collected a great array of miscellaneous facts. His belief on education was that the aim of formal schooling was not to learn many facts. This could be gotten from books. But to think ... to think with the tools of the scientific method ... that was the thing to be respected most in the intellectual ability of a person.

It was surprising to me how people were always sending them gifts from all over the country. And these were gifts from people they never heard of. One day, while I was there, a case containing six one-gallon cans of maple syrup arrived from Vermont, from some minister there. They were debating about what they could do with a case of six gallons of syrup like that, and they took one out of the case and gave it to me.

Another time a letter arrived. Some lady was offering him a gift of an Amate violin. Her husband had died and left it. And I told him that I thought that was just wonderful, as I knew they were really fine violins.

And he said, "But I could not accept this."

And I said, "Why not?"

"Well, I am but an amateur violinist. An instrument such as this should be in the possession of a really deserving artist. Such an instrument is not for me."

And we couldn't persuade him! He felt that it should be presented to someone who really deserved the instrument. But, if that were me, I'd have an Amate worth only about twenty thousand dollars!

Also, his mail arrived by the bushel. I saw letters from the far corners of the earth—from students, from scientists, from reports of work being done by colleagues. The task of answering them must have been tremendous. And a large portion of this mail, I happened to know, were letters begging for help on the part of persecuted Jews and Gentiles from Germany. This distressed him tremendously.

They helped so many people come over and escape from Germany—It's unbelievable. And as you know, he asked me to take care of one of these persons, a Dr. Elfenbein who had escaped from Germany into Switzerland. He was a famous expert in the field of international jurisprudence, and for whom I was successful in obtaining a grant for doing research in his particular field, through my friend Dr. Alan Gregg, who was head of the medical division of the Rockefeller Foundation.

# 13

# *An Unforgettable Evening of Chamber Music*

And now I must tell you of a never-to-be forgotten gathering that took place in my home one evening. You should remember something about this, Joan, because you were there.

I have always tried to make our home a meeting place for learned people. Well, on this evening, I think I attained the ultimate in this direction. I told the Einstein's that along with the quartet players, I was having a social evening, and there would be present some very interesting personalities.

Well, the whole family agreed to come. So you can imagine having present in our home at one time: Dr. Albert Einstein, his stepson Dr. Harry Einstein, his sister Mrs. Maja Winterler, his secretary Miss Helen Dukas, his mathematician Dr. Valentine Bargmann, Dr. William Mayer, Professor of Psychiatry at the University of Berlin for fifteen years, and his very gifted wife, Elizabeth Mayer, who translated the works of Goethe from the German into English, Professor Salter, political science professor at the University of Wisconsin, his wife Catherine, poetess for the anti-Nazi League, Benjamin Britten, already famous as a composer, Peter Pears, one of England's greatest tenors, and the quartet consisting of Uncle Milton Samuel, Howard Koch, and Eamons.

Also present was Joseph Scharl, the fine artist (*who painted the portrait that was featured on the Hofstra University Einstein Centennial poster.*)

And the music on that evening was just unbelievably beautiful! First of all, you played on the piano, Joan. Dr. Einstein thought that you were very talented. I think you played a Beethoven Sonata.

Then Britten and Pears performed some German Lieder, which the Einstein's, I could see, were enjoying every second.

The quartet played some trios. Dr. Bargmann was a fabulous pianist. Einstein said of him, "Not only is he the world's greatest mathematition, but he is also one of the world's greatest pianists."

Then Dr. Bargmann played the Dachnanyi Quintette.

After that, we sat around and had some coffee and cake. However, Professor Salter had a camera, and he was snapping pictures all over the place to the point that it was very annoying. And poor Professor Einstein was sitting at the table trying to eat cake and have some coffee, and just about every time the coffee cup would reach his lips, Professor Salter would shoot a question at him: "What do you think of this?" "What do you think of that?"

Einstein would make a few remarks and then lift the cup to his mouth again when Salter would say, "What about that?" And he'd have to drop the cup again. The cup kept coming up and down and poor Einstein couldn't drink the cup of coffee no-how! It was very annoying.

I saved the situation by asking Professor Salter a few questions so that I could get him off Einstein's back.

It was really a scintillating, stimulating and exciting evening. Finally it came time for all of us to go home. I took the Einstein's in my car, and as we were driving to Nassau Point, I said to him, "Well, Professor, on this night my home was greatly honored."

And he said, "But how could your home know this?"

And I laughed. It was almost midnight!

He said to me, "Now would be a good time, if we go inside the house, and we go to work on this problem about the contraction of a rod."

I said, "But it's almost midnight, and Miss Dukas will be after me."

He said, "Then we make it Sunday afternoon at 2:00 P.M."

So we had a date!

There were other evenings like that. Practically none of Professor Salter's pictures turned out. The camera was set wrong! I wasn't sorry—He should have known better than to be so annoying.

Benjamin Britten was very fond of and much engrossed with Bobby (*my brother, Bob Rothman*), and while all this was going on, Britten disappeared. We found him upstairs later, in Bobby's room, working on building model airplanes. Isn't that just like Ben?

Some time later, I sent a picture of Professor Einstein and Dr. Bargmann standing together to Dr. Bargmann, and he wrote me the following letter:

Dear Mr. Rothman,

With great pleasure I remember the charming musical soirées at your house, and I hope that some day they may be repeated. A copy of the photograph I sent to my parents. They live in Lithuania, and they liked it very much. My best wishes for a Happy New Year.

Very sincerely yours,

Valentine Bargmann
December 30, 1939

An Unforgettable Evening of Chamber Music 95

*Here is the photo that Dad referred to:*

Dr. Albert Einstein and Dr. Valentine Bargmann
Photo by David Rothman

# 14

## *Dealing with Crowds*

Here's quite a story. One summer night, there was to be a mass meeting at the Southold Fire House to discuss the proper way to care for the increasing number of Christian refugees fleeing Hitler's Germany. The committee in charge wondered if I could induce Einstein to come, figuring that his presence would insure good attendance and much interest. For a cause like that, I knew I could get him to come, and so it was arranged.

That evening I wore a white jacket, and when I arrived to pick up Einstein and Miss Dukas, he said, "My, how elegant you are!"

He was wearing a gray sweater, white duck pants, and the inevitable white piece of rope around his waist for a belt. While I was passing a few words with Miss Dukas, he disappeared, and when he reappeared, I could see he had made a concession. Now he was wearing a gray jacket instead of the sweater!

Then I noticed a little white something near his mouth that looked like a white particle of food, so I made a motion with my hand as if to brush it off.

He dived his head, and said something that sounded like, "Schav!" But I didn't understand and tried again. Again he ducked.

The next time he made a swift, slapping motion at my hand. If I hadn't been fast enough, he would have slapped it, but good!

"Schav!" he said, louder. Then it dawned on me that he was saying, "Shave!" and I realized that he had nicked himself with the razor and put a dab of Noxema on it. This is how I discovered that he could get angry, too, gentle as he seemed. But was I embarrassed! I tell you, I felt like two cents!

At any rate, we drove to the village, and I parked in our back yard, intending to walk with him the short distance to the firehouse. As we walked along on the street, I could see that people were staring at us. As we neared the firehouse, I noticed Supreme Court Judge L. Baron Hill standing at the entrance.

I said to Einstein, "I see the Judge of the Suffolk Country Supreme Court standing by the door. Would you like me to introduce you to him? Or do we just walk in without doing things like that? I thought I might check with you."

He said, "If it is customary to introduce one to the Judge, by all means let us do it."

So I introduced him to Judge Hill, and we went upstairs and sat down. There was a large crowd already, and the meeting got underway.

There wasn't much chance of being treated in a natural way! Reverend Palmer, who was on the platform with the speakers, came down and asked Professor Einstein if he would sit with the speakers. Before we could do anything about it or say a word, the Professor got up and agreed, and sat on the platform. This, I knew, we hadn't counted on.

To top it off, after the speakers, without a word of warning, they called on Professor Einstein to say a few words. I felt terrible! But he got up and in one sentence said a lot more than the speakers who had talked on and on and gotten nowhere.

He said, "You must organize. We Jews have had for a long time organizations equipped to handle these situations. You Christians must do likewise if you would avoid much suffering on the part of your brethren."

With that, he stepped down from the platform and sat down beside me. People stood up then and, lo and behold, they all started to crowd around me and Einstein and Miss Dukas, with requests:

"Introduce me, Dave, introduce me!"

I said, "Please, please, act natural! This isn't the thing to do. Just let these people act like ordinary people. Don't push and don't shove."

One woman said, "Well, Dave, if you won't introduce me, I'll introduce myself."

And she stuck her hand out to Professor Einstein and said, "Professor, I'm from Europe, too."

He looked a little surprised and said, "Well, that's quite interesting."

Then he put his mouth down to my ear and said, "*Get me oudt of here!*"

Well, then I began to work my elbows. I really became concerned and I made a path for him through the crowd. I was quite relieved when I was able to get him out of that building. And we started to walk down to our house when out from behind a tree dodged a man and it was Dr. Gambi Robinson, who was once dean of John's Hopkins University.

He said, "Dave, introduce me to the Professor. I know a mutual friend."

Well, I felt this man was worth introducing, and I introduced him. He told Einstein that the friend was Simon Flexner, who was somehow involved in bringing Einstein over to the Institute for Advanced Study in Princeton, NJ, and we had a few words.

Then we continued on our walk to the house. As we walked, I told him a little story about Gambi Robinson—how one night there was a carnival in town, and he went up there and was fleeced of his money. He ran into the store and asked me to lend him $100.

I said, "What in the world would you want $100 for?"

He answered, "I lost all my money down at the carnival, and I want to try to win it back."

I said, "Oh, no you don't!"

I called the police department and told them about this. They went to the carnival and got Robinson back his money.

I said to Einstein, "What a business man that was!"

He replied, "You know, if we are to be good business men, we cannot be good scientists!"

When we reached the front of the house, Miss Dukas said, "I must go into the drug store to buy something. You'd better stay here with Mr. Rothman because people will look on you."

I said, "Let's go in the house. There's nobody home, and we'll wait inside."

He thought that was a good idea, so we walked in. I opened the door, and lo and behold, there were at least 35 of my friends sitting all over the living room, sitting on the stairs. Every chair was taken. I was absolutely amazed.

It seems that these people had come from Riverhead and as far as Center Moriches, and they thought it would be nice if they stopped in to see me! And so I introduced Einstein to everyone.

The first one was the Rabbi, who was nearest. I heard Einstein say, "Oh, a Rabbi!" He started to relate a funny story to him, while I greeted the guests. I saw that he got along beautifully. He mingled around, and seemed to be right at home.

I was surprised at that. Then I left the whole gang at the house. Professor Einstein and Miss Dukas got into the car, and I drove them down to Nassau Point. I told him how I was as much surprised as he must have been when we opened the door and suddenly saw this bunch of people there.

He laughed and said, "Well, you could not know this."

Then I left, and came back to Southold to visit with my friends. In a way I was quite pleased with the turn of events. I felt that all of these friends of mine must have felt good about having met Einstein. I'm sure they felt it was quite an experience for them.

# 15

## *Another historic close call*

Professor Einstein once remarked to me, "Quartet playing, and sailing: They are the noblest pleasures."

Well, I'll tell you about a bit of sailing ... I wonder if he felt that way about this particular sail!

He asked me if I could suggest a place to store the sailing boat. *(The boat was named Tiniff, which means "junk" in Yiddish!)* I suggested our back yard, since we had plenty of room. But how to get it there? After some discussion, we decided that he would sail it from his beach in Nassau Point to the head of Town Creek.

Well, one sunny morning, Miss Dukas called me and informed me that the Doctor had left at 9:30 A.M. sailing, with his sister Maja, to my home.

"Okay," I said, and told her I would advise her when they arrived. I had no idea how long this would take, but comes 2 P.M. and I was beginning to wonder. Comes 3 P.M., no sign of them, and I was more concerned. Comes 4 P.M., still no word, and I was getting alarmed. Five P.M., no word, and now I was really scared. I took the car and drove to Founder's Landing, and scanned the water. No sailboat was in sight. I sped to Cedar Beach; no sign of them there. Then down to Town Harbor Road; still no sign.

Soon it was 6 o'clock, and I was really frightened, having visions of all sorts of accidents, cursing myself for letting him venture into such an arrangement. I raced home, intending to call for help from the police and the Coast Guard, because it was getting dark. I was just about to pick up the phone when it rang: "Hey, Dave, this is Captain Meyer. There's a wild-looking couple with white hair who need haircuts, asking how to sail a boat to your house. I can hardly understand them. They're down here at Founder's Landing." Boy, was I glad to hear that!

The first thing I did was to call Tony Slatka, who works in Goldsmith's boatyard. I asked him to take the shop boat around to Founder's Landing and tow the *Tiniff* in rather than to have them sail it down the creek. I jumped in the car and headed down to Founder's Landing. There I found them. Einstein's pants were rolled up, his feet knee deep in water ... the professor and his sister ... pushing the sailboat out into the water, intending to sail it up the creek. I had them pull the boat back and I saw Tony coming around with the boat shop tender. We left Tony in charge and I brought Einstein and Maja back to the house.

Before I left, I alerted Pauline (Dobeck), who was our maid then, and Emma to have hot food ready, and to phone Miss Dukas.

We went down to the Town Creek and Tony was just about coming in with their boat. When they pulled it up on shore, Tony started to pull the mast out. Well, there was a little American flag the Einstein's had at the top of the mast. As Tony was pulling the mast out, the flag slipped out somehow and fell into the mud. I saw Einstein rush forward, right into the mud, and promptly pick up the flag. He wiped it off carefully. I saw him rolling it up neatly and I felt this showed the deep respect he had for our country. It moved me because I saw it fall, and I thought nothing of it, while Einstein rushed forward to pick it up.

Then we went home, and the food was set out in the dining room. Was I relieved! They were simply starved. He seemed to think nothing of it at all. He said they had almost reached Greenport before they realized that they had gone too far east, and that they had sailed passed Southold. None of us realized how many hazards were involved, and I still shudder when I think of the situation.

*I remember that Einstein was upset that we were having dinner in the dining room, because that was so formal and he didn't want to be treated as a famous guest. He thought it was too much fuss! Dad finally convinced him that we were eating in the dining room because that was the only table big enough for Dad, Emma, my brother Bob and me, Maja and Einstein to dine at!*

*When Einstein arrived, I was playing cards with friends at the kitchen table. It was then that Einstein greeted us and gave us the riddle about how high one could jump on the moon.*

*A lovely meal was served, and tragedy was averted.*

*Years later, Dad and Mother bought a cabin cruiser, and Dad took courses in boating from the Peconic Bay Power Squadron. He learned about currents and ETA's (estimated times of arrival), charts, navigating courses, and so on. If he had taken the courses before 1939, he* never *would have suggested such a trip in that small boat, with no food and water. There are many perils on that course, which leads past Paradise Point with its strong currents. It's lucky that Dr. Einstein arrived at all!*

# 16

## *Our Walks Together*

One day while we were hiking around the woods at Nassau Point, I asked him, "Tell me: How in the world did you hit on the idea of Relativity, anyway? What line of thinking led you to such conclusions?"

He thought a while, and then he answered, "You know, when we realized the equivalence of inertial and gravitational mass, I had the first clue I needed."

Then he started to explain what was meant by this equivalence, but it was more than I could grasp at the time. He seemed to be sad about this, because I couldn't follow him. He told me how things began to fit into place—to fit together—of his excitement, which was such that he could hardly stand it. He couldn't sleep or eat for days, and really got sick. Now you can see the wonderment in my own face as he was telling me this, in that picture where we are walking together on the road.

2. Walking at Nassau Point

Photo by Reginald Donahue

The thought of ferreting out from this great mind the birth of these new, great, most radical concepts in the field of human knowledge, which gave mankind a totally new concept of the nature of the universe, caused me no end of excitement.

I awoke the next morning to find I understood what he meant by inertial and gravitational mass. At least, I thought so. I called to tell him and he really was pleased.

So the next day, I went down to Nassau Point, and again we proceeded to talk about these things, taking on where we left off. This contact with him was one of the things that still gives me a great sense of deep excitement.

In spite of all the time we spent together, walking and in my home, I never pointed a camera at him or any of the family. I felt that would not be the natural thing to do. While in our home, I saw that he was at ease, and seemed to revel in the natural home-life atmosphere. He'd kibitz with you kids, and always seemed at ease. His whole family came several times for dinner. Also, several times his grandson, Hadi, came to spend the day with Bobby around the place. Also, Mrs. Winteler came to play duets with your Aunt Regina.

On one occasion I said to Dr. Einstein, while he was here at the house, "Soon it will be time for you to go back to Princeton, and all this will become a memory, with nothing concrete to keep the experience alive in our minds ... like pictures."

"Oh," he said, "This can easily be remedied. Come tomorrow, and bring your camera, and we will take pictures."

So I asked Reginald Donahue *(a local photographer)* to come along with me, to take pictures of us as we walked around together. You know the results. You remember the picture of us sitting on the rock together. Under my arm was a copy of the New York Times. I wanted to get rid of it, so I threw it towards the beach.

Well, the wind caught it, and separated the sheets, and they flew and scattered in all directions, all over the beach.

Einstein said, "Look, you have soiled the beach!" And he started chasing after the papers, and I along with him, until we picked up every bit.

There is one picture of us carrying the crushed sheets of paper. Such were his feelings about littering the beach and our country side.

Photo by Reginald Donahue

Reg Donahue did a beautiful job of taking the pictures, as he inconspicuously followed us around. When I showed them to the Einstein family one night, he came to the one of the two of us walking in the road.

He said, "In this one, I look like Adam walking in the Garden of Eden!"

They all liked them, and I sent a set to his son, Dr. Harry Einstein, who wrote me that they were the best pictures taken of his father in recent years.

Photo by Reginald Donahue

*Here's the photo of Einstein sitting on a rock, taken by Reginald Donahue during one of their walks at Nassau Point:*

*Albert Einstein clowning with the violin in the Rothman living room in 1939. This photo appeared at the Smithsonian Centennial Exhibit in 1979 with credits to David Rothman, my father, who took the photo.*

When I pointed the camera at Mrs. Winterler, she said, "Why would you take pictures of me? I am not famous like my brother."

I was about to say that "I would like to remember you, too, along with your brother," but I sensed that she just didn't like to be photographed. Hence I quickly desisted, and therefore I have no photos of her or the others. I sensed a similar reaction from all of them.

There was one group pose of his whole family and of our whole family, posed in the living room. He said, "Ah, this one I should like a copy of." It didn't come out, and I've been heartbroken about that for years. He seemed so anxious for it. That was just like him.

I think I should tell you this: Great a man as he was, gentle, humble, as is his reputation, I happen to know that he could be quite as human as the rest of us. He couldn't get along with his son-in-law, Margot's husband, at all. Margot and Mrs. Winterler told me that they couldn't be together in the room for ten minutes before they started quarreling violently. Miss Dukas told me they were like a pair of game cocks when near each other. And they all felt very badly about this. In fact, this was why Margot was here in America without her husband.

I found, whenever you were in his presence, your reasoning always had to be logical. He disliked trivialities in conversation. He loved a good, logical discussion, on almost any subject. If you said something illogical, he would just stop conversing, put his pipe in his mouth, and walk away from you, into another room sometimes. I've seen that happen.

If he started an explanation about something, he made a condition beforehand: "If you do not follow me step by step, you must stop me. Otherwise we get hopelessly confused. You must not say I understand if you know you do not." And believe me, I was careful about that! In other words, he expected sincerity in ones desire to understand. And if he recognized sincerity in you, he would go to great lengths to help you.

# 17

## *A Lesson in Relativity*

At 2 o'clock one Sunday afternoon, I arrived at his home as he had suggested. I found a house full of guests there. When I came in, he seemed pleased to see me and seemed oblivious to the guests. He went out on the porch with me.

I felt a little uneasy about that, thinking maybe I should beg off and come at another time. But immediately he asked me to sit down beside him, picked up a pad and a pencil, and started in with the questions I had asked him.

First, he stated the usual caution.

"You must stop me if you do not understand."

And I agreed.

But I said to him, "I, too, must make a condition. You must not resort to mathematics," And he agreed.

Then he called out a Dr. Gustav Bucky. This Dr. Bucky was a famous scientist in his own right, in the field of X-ray radiation, and had a ray called "The Bucky Ray," named (of course) after him. Einstein wanted him to join us so that he could demonstrate to him that a layman, in fact a mere merchant, could comprehend these problems.

First he said to me, "You know, I use no instruments. My tools are simply a pad and a pencil. This is all I have ever needed."

Well, from two until five o-clock we were at it, but I got nowhere in trying to grasp what he wanted me to. The whole pad was full of mathematical symbols. I didn't complain about that, but I tore off the sheet he was using, and I still have it to show how he was explaining to me, "without the use of mathematics," the problem of the change of the rhythm of clocks and the contraction of rods in space.

He seemed so sad at his failure that I felt quite bad about it. I supposed he was so accustomed to the use of mathematical symbols in his thinking about things that unconsciously, he resorted to the use of math in the explanation of any problem.

*Dad told me that later that evening, he suddenly felt that he understood the explanation. He called Einstein to tell him, and Einstein was extremely pleased!*

*Many years later, in 1979, my Dad was invited to be the keynote speaker at Hofstra University for the Einstein Centennial Celebration, speaking about "Einstein as a Human Being." This amused him greatly, because he had attended school only as far as the eighth grade, and here he was speaking to college professors and scientists!*

*Dad described to the impressive group of scholars and scientists the events of the remarkable evening in 1939, when Einstein drew on a sheet of paper, without the use of mathematics, his simplified (for him) calculation, explaining to my father why a rod contracts in the direction of the motion as it approaches the speed of light. Dad didn't understand the mathematics, but he kept that paper. He would hand out copies of the document, and the scientists were really thrilled to have a copy of this amazing document, in Einstein's own handwriting!*

112  MY FATHER AND ALBERT EINSTEIN

*This document was sold in 2003, along with the letters, to Profiles in History, a firm in California. They had the calculation sheet analyzed, and it was shown to be an abbreviated Theory of Relativity in Einstein's own handwriting:*

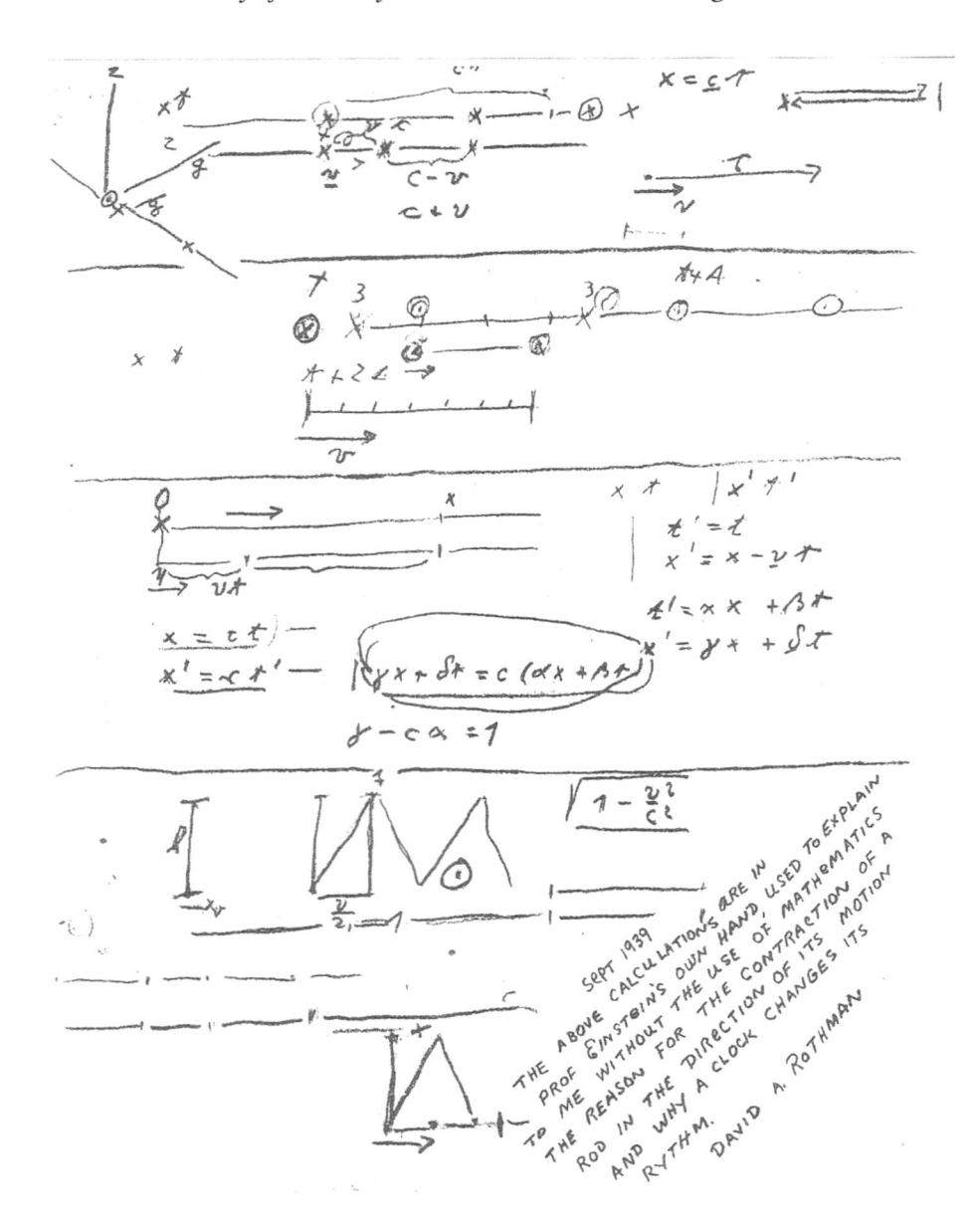

*A Lesson in Relativity*     113

*The poster for that occasion showed a painting of Einstein by the artist, Joseph Scharl. Scharl was a fine artist who had come to the United States from Europe during World War II, and he was struggling financially. Therefore, a group was formed to contribute $3.00 a month toward Scharl's financial expenses! In return, each supporter received a painting. My sister has a beautiful painting by Joseph Scharl that shows the bright fall foliage of the Hudson River banks.*

*See page 114 for another of Scharl's painting of Einstein that was used for the Hofstra Einstein Centennial in 1979.*

I don't know what the other guests thought about our spending the whole afternoon secluded on the porch, leaving the rest of them in the house there. But there was nothing I could do about it. I must admit that I felt somewhat flattered with his letting me monopolize his attention all afternoon, to the exclusion of all the other guests.

You know, when we were together, all the time we were together, we never engaged in trivial conversation. We always discussed something that was interesting and stimulating, and I must say, he seemed to enjoy it just as much as I did. That, too, is a great source of satisfaction to me.

I can't remember who it was, but someone told me that he was somehow related to Einstein, and asked me to mention this to him, which I did. Einstein said to me, "I do not know such a one. You know, since I have become so famous, my relatives have reached astronomical proportions."

I told Einstein that Joseph Scharl was my friend. Scharl had once painted Einstein's portrait. However, Einstein did not recall Scharl, and said, "Did he paint me for MY edification or for his own?"

It seems he often sat for artists who needed a little push along the road to success, so they could claim they painted him.

Finally, when I arranged for Scharl to meet Einstein in our home, Einstein did remember Scharl, and they became very friendly. Scharl used to go to Princeton once a month to visit him regularly, right until he died. And you will remember, Joan, how Scharl told you about it, when you once visited him in New York City.

*Joseph Scharl lived a few doors down from Juilliard on Claremont Avenue, so I stopped in one day in about 1949. Scharl painted the wonderful portrait of Einstein that appeared on the poster for the Hofstra College Einstein Centennial Exhibit, in 1979. I and my siblings all have framed copies of that poster in our living rooms!*

*Here is a copy of that poster:*

When Scharl visited Einstein in Princeton, Dr. Einstein always asked him "why Mr. Rothman did not come, too." On every occasion, when I ran into Scharl, he was always asking me why I didn't go to Princeton, and that Dr. Einstein was always asking for me, and why I didn't come.

I, of course, felt good about that, and I feel sorry that I didn't go; but I didn't want to take him away from his work. That's the way it was.

I also arranged for Hans Kavnatzky, who lived in Indian Neck in Peconic, to meet him. Kavnatzky sculptured a bust of Dr. Einstein that I thought was very good, but I don't know what became of it. As you remember, Kavnatsky's house burned down, and he was inside and lost his life in the fire. I never found out where that bust went to. It was a sad thing.

People around here got to know on what nights the string quartet would be playing, and a good crowd would be standing around outside our house, listening to the music through the windows, or hoping to catch a glimpse of him. I always sneaked him in and out through the back yard.

A woman told me she brought her grandchild each time, and once she spotted us getting out of the car, and they saw him. The experience was one that would always be one of the most important events of their lives, she told me.

I remember so well, and so vividly, when these musical evenings came to an end, he would say to me with such deep feeling, putting an arm about my shoulders, "It was beautiful."

Boy, what memories, Joan! He was so sincere, so genuine in his friendship. He showed such deep, genuine interest in Emma and in all you kids ... always wanted to know all the details of what was happening every day.

I recall at one time one of the Einstein family had an upset stomach. Not being familiar with the medical situation around here, they called me on the phone and asked me if I could recommend a good doctor who I felt would be satisfactory to them.

So I called a Dr. Lenowitz, who went down there and took care of things. I don't know if you remember him, Joan, but he was the doctor who lived in Cutchogue, a very good friend of ours.

Later in the day, I dropped around to see how things were with them, and to see if there was anything I could do. Everything was fine, and they told me they liked the doctor very much.

By the way, the Einstein's had a little Airedale dog around the house. I watched Einstein feeding it himself. They evidently liked pets. They had a beautiful cat in Princeton, and a cage with a hamster. His home had a really "homey" atmosphere.

On this day, this little incident took place:

While we were sitting around chatting, it got a little cool in the room, so Einstein started to close one of those long, wide doors, which shut off part of the room, which would make it a little warmer.

As the door was being pushed along by Einstein, their little dog, a wire-haired terrier, would always begin to bark wildly, running alongside the moving door, biting and scratching at the leading edge of the door.

I noticed that the dog always got excited when the door was being closed. The paint on the edge of the door was already scratched off from his claws and teeth. This time Einstein looked at me and said, "I wonder why this dog always does this. Do you suppose he can see that the door is contracting in the direction of its motion, and that he does not know what to make of it, and it makes him angry?"

You see how relaxed and informal he could be with me. This is quite typical of how we were together. Of course, you must understand what he meant by the door contracting in the direction of its motion; you do, otherwise you wouldn't know what he was talking about!

One evening we were on the way home from one of our quartet session. Mrs. Winteler and Miss Dukas were in the car with us. Something in our conversation prompted me to pose this question:

"Why was it that such a disproportionately large percentage of Jewish men are found to be in the professions, considering the small numbers in relation to the total population? Was it the result of an innate superiority and capacity, or was it because Jewish young men had always had to face a hard struggle for existence and success throughout the ages, compared to men of other denominations? Did the constant struggling against a handicap throughout time, posed by intolerance, persecution, bigotry, and discrimination have something to do with it?"

Well, did I start something! At first they discussed this calmly; then things became more and more heated and excited, until they were all talking at once—believe it or not—and you know how much I dislike disorderly discussion. They even suddenly began talking in German. Miss Dukas apologized to me, and explained that they can think better in German.

I'm sorry to say I never did learn what the answer to this problem was, or what they thought about it. We reached home before the discussion ended, and they probably carried it on in their house. So, you see, even around great minds like that, such things can happen. I never got a word in edgewise!

# 18

## *A Fond Farewell*

This next episode, to me, is the most memorable one of all.

The summer was about over and the time was approaching when they were due to leave for home. I wanted to be able to say "Good-bye" to them before they left and when last I was with them, I told them so and asked when would be a good time to drop by.

Well, strangely, they began to confer in German among themselves. Then they turned to me and Miss Dukas said, "After lunch."

I don't remember the particular day, but I knew that that day happened to be my birthday—September 14—and they were to leave on the 15$^{th}$.

So the day arrived and I went to their home. I knew I should not stay long, as they had lots of packing to do; so I soon started to take my leave and was about to say my "Good-bye," when Einstein approached me with a book in his hand, and with the others standing around me, presented it to me, with all of them wishing me Happy Birthday! I was just flabbergasted!

I could not imagine how they knew it was my birthday. I was sure I had never mentioned it to any of them.

Well, Emma, it seems, for my birthday had gotten the idea of ordering a book that had just come off the press, called "Einstein: The Maker of Universes" by Garbedian, one of the editors of *The New York Times*. She then gave it to Einstein to inscribe and told him to give it to me on my birthday.

So, you see, that was the reason for all the talk among themselves in German. On the front-piece of the book, he wrote in German, which translates as follows:

"May this book remind you of the happy times we spent together in the summer of 1939." He signed it simply, "A. Einstein."

On the adjoining page, all you kids wished me "Happy Birthday," followed by each of your signatures. This book happens to be one of my most prized possessions. Just get the significance of such a statement as he made here!

This is a man who is credited with some of the greatest intellectual and scientific achievements in the entire history of man, and in fact, was considered among the immortals at the tender age of 27. And for me to have been so privileged was amazing—for if he wrote it, he was the kind who would really mean it. And when I took his hand to say good-bye to him, he put one arm affectionately around my shoulder and said, "You know, this has been one of the most beautiful summers of my whole life, and this I owe to your initiative." His face lit up with a friendly gleam.

So, as I left him finally, I would have a hard time describing my feelings and emotions. This great man, who had said such a thing to me ... Wow!

So, they departed Nassau Point for 110 Mercer Street in Princeton, NJ. His "sailing boat," as he called it, was stored in our back yard. I didn't know it then, but they were never to come back here. From then on we corresponded with each other by letter.

George Russell Harrison, Dean of the School of Science of MIT, wrote an article in the *Atlantic Monthly* entitled "Albert Einstein." He deals with Einstein's greatness, and in this article he writes, "My most treasured possession is a single letter I have from him, in connection with a technical matter."

Well, I have about 25 letters ... not technical, but personal.

I thought some of taping the letters, but instead I will mention just some highlights. These letters are in my safe.

*In 2003, my brother Bob, my sister Em, and I finally sold those letters to "Profiles in History," a company in California. Some of the letters were more valuable than others.*

*After the letters were sent to California, "Profiles in History" must have sold them. Eventually, after the passage of a few months, the less valuable letters appeared for sale on E-Bay, and the grandchildren bought some of them back! Therefore, some of those letters are still in the Rothman family! Others were purchased by the Southold Historical Society.*

# 19

## *Letters*

I read a news item in The New York Times that someone had offered Einstein $50,000 if he would write for him, with Einstein's own hand, an exact copy of the original paper on the Special Theory of Relativity. I wrote Einstein about this and asked, "By the way, what did become of this paper? Was this too burned by the Nazi's along with the rest of your books?"

He answered, by letter: "My first manuscript about Relativity was not burned by the Nazi's. I myself threw it into the wastebasket after it was printed, judging it was good for nothing. At that time, I knew nothing of the snobbery of this human world."

Joan, this is a reference to one of the most important papers in the history of human thinking and scientific discovery.

April 14, 1944

Herrn David Rothmann
Southold L.I.N.Y.

Dear Mr. Rothman:

    I was quite thrilled when I saw the beautiful boat your son has build for himself and I am wishing him happy times in it. Your Bay is really the most beutiful sailing ground I ever experienced and I regret that the health of my family compells me to go into the mountains for recreation.

    My first manuscript about relativity was not burned by the Nazis. I myself threw it into the waste-basket after it was printed judging it was good for nothing. At that time I knew nothing of the snobbery of this human world.

    I feel quite satisfied with the progress of the war and especially with the strength of the Russians. I remember quite well how I trembled for them when Hitler began his attack in 1941.

    With kind wishes and greetings for you and your family

        yours sincerely,

        A. Einstein.

This is a letter of June 10, 1940:

"I am very sorry that I have to miss the beautiful quartet evenings you arranged last year and also our talks. I send my greetings to the quartet brothers and to you and your family.
Cordially yours,
A. Einstein."

July 20, 1940: "Dear Mr. Rothman,

"I was really touched when I received your kind gift *(a pair of sandals)*. I feel happy indeed about your kindness, and at the same time ashamed because I could not show my gratitude for all your care in connection with my boat. I am sailing daily with my sister, and I am homesick when I think of the beautiful musical evenings.

"With kind regards to you, your family, and the musical friends, Very sincerely, A. Einstein."

Each year, I sent him a gift of those "sundahls" which he liked so much, and that is what he referred to as the "kind gift."

January 8, 1941: "I am thinking often of the beautiful hours we spent together in the last years and I feel very grateful for your kind patronage of my sailboat, 'Tiniff,' which is now on Saranac Lake. Wishing you and your family good luck for 1941, I am, Cordially yours, etc."

September 24, 1939: "I hope you are feeling well and are enjoying the fine autumn weather. Everybody is sending you the best and kindest regards. We hope that some day you will pay us a visit in Princeton."

This was written shortly after they left Peconic. It was signed by the secretary, Helen Dukas. *(Thirteen letters were typed on Einstein's typewriter, which was easily identified, and signed by Dr. Einstein. Other letters were apparently handled by the secretary, Miss Dukas.)*

December 3, 1942: I had written to them about Emma's wedding (November 26, 1942) in New York City. I told them that I realized it would be almost impossible for them to come, but I felt I wanted them to know that it was taking place.

I received this letter: "Heartiest congratulations to you, Mrs. Rothman and the young couple, and my best wishes for their happy future.

"I am very satisfied about the war news, and can imagine that you are feeling the same. Cordially, A. Einstein"

Then, at the bottom of this letter, is a note which reads, "My sincerest wishes, too, for you all and the young couple. Signed, "Maja Winterler." *(His sister.)*

On January 12, 1941, I had planned to visit them, and had written that I was coming.

He wrote, "The whole family will be delighted to see you again, and to meet Mrs. Rothman. Thursday afternoon around 3 o'clock will be convenient. If you don't write to the contrary, we will expect you then."

I couldn't make that trip, and also disappointed them on several other occasions, after promising to come. (*I think that this had something to do with the weather or illness in the family.*)

At another time, I noticed that they were having a dinner in New York City in his honor, and some very important people would be present. I read that he would be unable to come, and was ill and that arrangements had been made for him to deliver his speech by telephone.

I became a little concerned, and wrote to ask if there was anything I could do, and if so, I would come over right away.

I received this letter dated November 3, 1942:

"It is very kind of you to be concerned about my health, and to write me such a nice letter. In reality, my health is not so bad. I am only unable to attend dinners and other such social occasions outside Princeton. Even a person of strong health could not stand it in the long run. I am very glad that I and my 'Tiniff' have found such good and worthy successors, and I wish them both a good wind and fine trips.

"Cordially yours, A. Einstein"

He was referring to the fact that I wrote that Bobby had acquired a Star sailboat, and was sailing on Peconic Bay.

October 8, 1941: "I am happy to tell you that Margot has recovered beautifully. (*I think that Margot had asthma and allergies. The humidity on Long Island was not beneficial for her, so she was advised to vacation in the mountains.*) I am also well, and have been working very much. I shall be happy any time that you can find it possible to visit me here. Best wishes, etc."

(*Unknown date):* "Dear Mr. Rothman,

"It was very kind of you to send me again, this year, a gift of my favorite sandals. I cannot wear them yet because those you have given me last year are still of kingly elegance. I wear them always, in the sailboat and out.

"There is now more hope that Hitlerism will be destroyed; at any rate, a remarkable change since last year. Hoping you and your family are in the best of health, etc."

These excerpts, I think show the depth and intimacy of our friendship. You know, I don't think that more than half a dozen people in the entire world shared this privilege. There were hundreds of people who knew him, and came into contact with him as colleagues, but they never had an intimate friendly basis with him. Kings and Princes moved Heaven and Earth to get him to their social functions, to no avail; but if I asked him to drop around, he never failed to come.

# 20

# *A Visit to Albert Einstein in Princeton*

One of the saddest things of my life was that Mom was unable to be around to join me in this great experience. The women of the family would have loved her, for she was just like them in many ways. They were always busy knitting, tatting, making all sorts of handiwork. They, too, loved flowers and had their gardens; and you know how Mom loved flowers! Until we went to Princeton to visit them, they had never met her.

So, the time came when I felt we should pay them a visit in Princeton. I had disappointed them at least twice, but at last it was arranged that I should be there on a certain day. That day, when I awoke, there was the most beautiful covering of ice on all the trees, and roads; but I felt that this time, there could be no disappointment. That would really be an imposition. This time we felt that we must try, and if we found that we couldn't make it, we would just turn back.

We made it to New York all right. Instead of driving on to Princeton, we left the car in New York and took the train.

They were much surprised to see us, the weather being what it was. Promptly, they brought out hot tea and cake, and the ladies went off by themselves, chatting about the things ladies chat about.

They took to Mom as I knew they would. As for myself, I felt that I would like to sit around and not get too serious in conversation ... just get the news and relax with him. Einstein took me into his study and showed me his view of the flower garden from the studio window.

But it was not to be as I hoped. Whenever we two got together, trivial talk seemed impossible. I had read sometime before that, since the advent of relativity, the universe was now considered not finite but unbounded, where prior to that it was considered to be infinite. This concept had always bothered me, so I asked him how it could be "finite but unbounded." This seemed a contradiction of terms.

Herbert Spencer would argue that either the finite or unboundedness would be in the realm of the unknowable. Well, for the next two hours, we sat at the table, tea and cake untouched, our heads together, he, with a pad and pencil in his hand, totally oblivious to the women and their doings, trying to get me to understand his position in the matter.

I finally said, "I simply cannot conceive of "finite" or "unbounded."

He finally said to me, "Ah, this is because of your finite mind and finite habit of thinking!"

Too soon the time came to leave, and that, I'm sorry to say, was the last time I would see him alive. This loveable, saint-like, modest, humble, kindly person whom I knew, always looked with puzzled sorrow on the greatness which rushed upon him, because it deprived him of the one thing in life that he yearned for most: simple friendship. That was Albert Einstein, the man as I knew him, and as very few others recognized him. Few treated him as a human being. I'm glad that I did.

# 21

## *The End of the Story*

*After so very many years, Mother began writing again in "Our Diary." Mother spelled words literally, the way they sounded, just as Nana did, and I may follow her example! One can also recognize the effects of Mother's breakdowns, I think, in the way that she writes at this time.*

### March 17th, 1951

It's almost 30 years since my last entry was made and I just guess I was so busy bringing up our family that I forgot to enter our busy, sometimes happy, sometimes sad, happenings. I shall try to recall a few as time goes on and not wait so long between entries.

### October 31, 1951

Dear Diary,

Much has transpired since I last recorded in this—our weaver of a Dream Life. It is a gusty, rainy day and just the sort of mood for retrospect. In the days to come I shall try to catch up with the many things that have happened in the course of our lives.

The main thing seems to be that I have weathered two nervous breakdowns, the first, some twelve years ago and which lasted almost two years before I was normal again. The other happened last June, as a matter of fact, since the death of Aunt Regina on May 6th, 1951. Her long illness and the burden it put on me—above all else—seemed to have caused this set-back. However, I can really see myself fast coming back to normalcy once more; miraculously—for it was a great struggle and mostly will power on my part that brought back to life, as it were, a very sick woman. I have at last passed my menopause and that should help me a lot to keep my equilibrium.

My family has quite grown up and from here on the grandchildren, my devoted husband and many sincere friends will make it important for life to go on.

Until time warrants, I shall say "Adieu!"

## Saturday, November 3, 1951

It has been raining all day and night, but is most restful; for I have been able to go through all my various past letters from the family and in short order will make a preface to all these many years past, and also catch up to date. The main news now is that I am awaiting the birth of our 3$^{rd}$ grandchild, which is due in the next 3 weeks—our baby's (Joan). *(That refers to me. I was married to wonderful Bob Brill and lived in East Hampton, NY where Bob helped his parents, Oscar and Gussie Brill run their clothing store,* Oscar Brill's.*)*

*Mother had many entries in her Diary, the last one dated April 1, 1961, when her youngest sister, Jeanette Samuel Loeb Dennis died of staph pneumonia.*

## April 1$^{st}$, 1961

Too bad, dear diary, I have to again record a sorrow. Jeanette *(Samuel Loeb Dennis)* passed away on Monday, March 27$^{th}$ after 2 days of pneumonia. My loss is forever for this link of family was closest of all. I have lost a real sister as well as the last one. Since her family are the greatest losers, I shall accept what comes and thank God for all my blessings. May there be many years before another sorrowful moment, which has to come with life. Each day is a treasure from here on, so must be lived as the last one anyway. Since doing for others is the best medicine, I hope to find peace of mind in this alone. R.R.

January 12, 1978

SIXTIETH ANNIVERSARY--Mr. and Mrs. David Rothman of Southold celebrated their 60th wedding anniversary Saturday night. The Rothmans founded Rothman's Department Store on Main Street in Southold 59 years ago. Times photo by Scott Harris

*Both Mother and Dad had colon cancer during their 60's. Both were operated on successfully. Dad contracted acute leukemia at the age of 85. He died at St. Charles Hospital in Port Jefferson on November 19, 1981.*

*Mother was devastated, but she made new friends and continued to live in the house attached to Rothman's Dept. Store. In 1987 she was diagnosed with multiple myeloma (cancer of the bone marrow). She died at home under hospice care on May 23, 1987. I was with her.*

Albert Einstein and David Rothman sitting on a boat gunwale at Nassau Point, Long Island. Summer of 1939. Photo by Reginald Donahue

This shows Rothman's Department Store as it looks today, in Southold, New York
June 21, 2007
Photo by Joan Brill

The photo below shows Rothman's Department Store with its owners, Ronnie and Bob Rothman
June 21, 2007
Photo by Joan Brill

# APPENDIX A

## *The Einstein Miracles by Dr. Jerold M. Lowenstein*

*I was searching the Internet for information about Albert Einstein, and I came across this wonderful article. It seems to explain Einstein's life and theories in terms that the layman can understand. I e-mailed Dr. Jerold M. Lowenstein, and he gave me permission to use his article in any way that I wish. Therefore, I am affixing it to this narration. I thank Dr. Lowenstein, with deep gratitude.*

Counterpoints in science
This article appeared in the Magazine of the California Academy of Sciences.

### The Einstein Miracles

Jerold M. Lowenstein

The year 2005 marks the centenary of Albert Einstein's annus mirabilis (miracle year). That was the year the 26-year-old physicist proved that atoms are real, assembled the foundations of quantum physics, and changed our concepts of space, time, and motion with E=mc2, the world's most famous equation. As a result, Einstein is recognized by physicists as the most important scientific figure of the twentieth century. To this day, Einstein's name and theories still carry a magical quality even for those who have little idea of what it was he discovered.

One of the great unsolved questions Einstein tackled at the turn of the century was whether molecules were real or only a bookkeeping device to explain chemical reactions. In an attempt to quantify the existence of molecules, Einstein tested the concept of Brownian motion. Brownian motion, the random movement of microscopic particles suspended in a liquid or gas, had been observed for more than a century. When you look through a microscope at tiny particles like pollen in a liquid like water, the particles jiggle around, and no one understood why. Einstein proved mathematically that Brownian motion was due to the particles colliding with the water molecules and calculated how many molecules were present in the solution.

Einstein also changed the way we think about light. When light falls on certain metals, they eject electrons. Einstein explained the phenomenon by assuming that light consists of particles, or quanta (now called photons), rather than being purely a wave phenomenon as was previously thought. This work was the seed of quantum mechanics, which dominated twentieth-century physics and provided an understanding of atoms and the fundamental constituents of matter.

Despite his monumental contribution to this new field of study, Einstein rejected his quantum brainchild and its accompanying uncertainties. In quantum mechanics, one can only describe the probabilities of various outcomes. Einstein believed in "causality"-that if one knew enough about the present, one could predict the future precisely. "I do not believe that God plays dice," he said.

Prior to Einstein, scientists thought light was broadcast through a medium they called the ether, just as sound is transmitted through air. Ether was assumed to fill all of space in the same way that air fills a room. It was believed that the motion of the earth through the ether should create an "ether wind," just as a hand moving through the air creates a current. Hypothetically, light beams headed in the same direction as Earth should be carried along faster than light headed in other directions.

In 1887, American physicists Michelson and Morley went looking for the ether by clocking light headed in different directions. But whichever direction they measured it from, the velocity always came out the same. While the rest of the scientific world puzzled over these measurements, Einstein used them to create a radical new view of the universe-his theory of relativity.

If Michelson and Morley were right, Einstein realized, then one of physics' founding fathers was very, very wrong. Two centuries earlier, Sir Isaac Newton had stated that space was not only a fixed and infinite grid, but also that time was absolute, as if kept by a divine stopwatch. But if the velocity of light was constant, Einstein found, then time had to be relative. His "special theory of relativity" proved time is relative to the speed one is traveling at; five minutes to someone streaking by at thousands of miles an hour might be a lifetime to someone crawling at the speed of a turtle.

In this, Einstein was following in the footsteps of another great scientist, Isaac Newton. The two are often compared today. Newton's annus mirabilis was 1665, when he invented the calculus, explained how gravity works, discovered that white light contains the colors of the rainbow, and worked out the laws of motion. No one thought this brilliance could ever be equaled.

Newton conceived of a universe based on gravitational force. All matter in the universe-the stars, the planets, even you and I-attracts other matter, and this explains the motions of heavenly bodies, the seasons, night and day, the tides, and why Australians do not go flying off into space.

Einstein's theory of gravitation, presented to the world in 1915, went a step further. Einstein disputed Newton's theory, arguing that gravity was not a force but rather a warping of space-time. Instead of bodies being attracted to one another, Einstein envisioned a curved universe whose shape is dependent on the distribution of mass within it. Imagine space as a stretched trampoline. When something heavy—such as a dumbbell—is placed in the center of the trampoline, it dips. If you try to roll a ball along the surface, the ball will roll towards the center. Einstein imagined gravity working the same way, with spacetime acting as the trampoline and matter playing the role of the dumbbell.

Which man was right? At the time, it was difficult to tell. The differences between each theory's predicted effects on the observable universe were so tiny that even Einstein had a hard time thinking of the right experiment.

Einstein thought that measurements of starlight during an eclipse might do the trick. Gravitation according to Newton predicts that starlight passing by the sun should be deflected by 0.87 seconds of arc—one arc-second being equivalent to the diameter of a dime viewed from a mile away. According to Einstein, the deflection should be exactly twice the Newtonian value.

Arthur Eddington, an eminent astronomer at Cambridge University, put the theories to the test by observing a total eclipse of the sun on Principé Island. On November 6, 1919, Eddington announced his results at a joint meeting of the Royal Society of London and the Royal Astronomical Society, beneath a portrait of Newton. World War I had just ended, and chauvinism was running high. Not many in that room were rooting for the German Jewish challenger of the British icon.

Eddington solemnly announced that he had found exactly the deflection Einstein predicted. Legend has it that at a press conference later, a reporter asked the self-assured Eddington whether it was true that only three people in the world understood Einstein's theory. Eddington is supposed to have responded, "Who is the third?"

The next day the London Times broke the story about Newton's overthrow, and the Einstein legend began. He became a world-famous figure, and everywhere he went, mobs turned out to see and hear him.

Einstein said he wanted to know how God created the universe. Though he did not believe in a God who directly interferes in the affairs of men, he referred affectionately to Der Alte (the Old One) as the wise mentor whose thoughts and works he was trying to comprehend.

When someone reported measurements—later proven wrong—that the velocity of light was not constant after all, Einstein dismissed the report with the comment, "God is subtle but he is not malicious." And while Eddington was studying the eclipse, a student asked Einstein what he would do if the results did not support his gravitation theory. He replied, "I would feel sorry for dear old God. My theory is correct."

All his scientific life, Einstein was driven by a powerful desire to describe space, time, matter, energy, and forces such as electromagnetism with a single theory. He once said that the longing to behold such harmony is like that of a religious devotee or a person in love. He did succeed in unifying space and time, mass and energy, gravitation and inertia. He failed, however, in his attempts to unite gravitation and electromagnetism. No one since has succeeded in creating a unified theory either.

Einstein seems to have been born with an innate interest in science. By his own account, Einstein experienced two miracles during his childhood in Ulm, Germany. When he was four, his father showed him a compass. At the thought that some mysterious force lay hidden behind commonplace objects, he trembled and grew cold. At age twelve he had similar feelings after he was given a small book on Euclidean geometry. He referred to it as his holy book. From age 12 to 16 he taught himself calculus.

Einstein studied physics in Zurich but after graduation could not find a university job. He went to work for the patent office in Bern instead. This gave him plenty of time to think about the most major problems in physics, which had gathered like storm clouds at the turn of the nineteenth century.

In 1903, he married Mileva Maric, a Serbian fellow student of physics. He and Mileva had two sons, but the marriage was not a happy one. In 1919 he asked for a divorce, which she bitterly resisted. She demanded as a condition that he promise to give her his Nobel Prize money when and if he received that honor. When the prize came to him in 1921, he promptly turned the award money over to his ex-wife.

Albert and Elsa Einstein Lowenthal, his cousin, were married June 2, 1919 in Berlin, where he was then a professor. Unlike the bohemian Einstein, who cared very little about money, clothes, or possessions, she was thoroughly middle class. According to Einstein's friend Charlie Chaplin, "She frankly enjoyed being the wife of the great man and made no attempt to hide the fact." Another friend commented that Einstein seemed out of place in the midst of the beautiful furniture, carpets, and paintings Elsa had assembled.

Einstein was not as fortunate in love as in physics. On the death of his lifelong friend Michele Besso, he wrote, "What I most admired in him as a human being is the fact that he managed to live for many years not only in peace but also in lasting harmony with a woman—an undertaking in which I twice failed disgracefully."

In December 1932, after the rise of Hitler, Einstein left Berlin for America. He was offered a position at the newly established Institute for Advanced Study in Princeton, NJ, where he remained for the rest of his life. Though a lifelong pacifist, he sent Roosevelt the letter which initiated the creation of the atomic bomb. He didn't want German physicists, working under Heisenberg, to invent it first. When he spoke out against the rise of McCarthyism after the war (it reminded him of the early days of the Nazis), several congressmen wanted to take away his American citizenship.

Just after Einstein died in 1955, a spectacular cascade of discoveries in astronomy further verified his ideas: radio and X-ray sources, quasars, cosmic microwave background radiation, pulsars, black holes, and the accelerated expansion of the universe. Nowadays, Einstein's ghost presides over many astrophysics seminars that mull over new data streaming in from observatories and satellites.

George Bernard Shaw aptly called Einstein "a maker of universes," but Einstein never took himself as seriously as others did. The famous picture of him licking an ice cream cone, eyes bright and an aureole of gray hair framing his visage, depicts the counterpoint between his childish delight in ordinary things and his world-changing intelligence. Sometimes Princeton high school students would phone his listed home number to get help with their math homework, and he would oblige. It's reported he was once asked to solve a difficult problem and responded, "I'm no Einstein!"

A century after his miracle year, we live in a universe of science that Albert Einstein more than any other man constructed. The light of his intellect continues to shine in molecules too small to see and galaxies beyond the range of human sight or comprehension.

◆ ◆ ◆

**Jerold M. Lowenstein** is professor of medicine at the University of California, San Francisco. jlowen@itsa.ucsf.edu

# APPENDIX B
## *The Einstein Family*

Here are some of the people who are mentioned in my Dad's narration:

Albert Einstein b. March 14, 1879 in Ulm, Germany d. April 18, 1955 in Princeton, New Jersey

Mileva Maric—First wife of Albert Einstein. b. December 19, 1875 d. August 4, 1948 in Zurich, Switzerland

Albert and Mileva had three children: Liserl (born before they were married). She was given for adoption, and after that there was no information about her.

Dr. Hans Albert Einstein (The son Harry) b. 1904. d. July 26, 1973 in Woods Hole, MA. Hans Albert was a professor of hydraulic engineering in California. He married Frieda Knecht (Einstein). Their son was Bernhard Caesar Einstein. b. 1930. I think that his nick name was Hadi or Huddy, as mentioned in Dad's tape.

Eduard Einstein. b. 1910. Eduard was a psychoanalyst. He died of schizophrenia in an institution.

Elsa Einstein Lowenthal—A cousin and second wife of Albert Einstein. b. 1876 d. 1936, shortly before Dad's narration occurs. Elsa nursed Dr. Einstein back to health during a time that he was very ill. After that, the two were married. This was Elsa's second marriage. Her first husband was Rudolf Max Lowenthal b. 1864 d. 1914. They had a daughter:

Margot (Einstein) Lowenthal. B. 1899. d. 1986.

Maja Einstein Winterler—Albert Einstein's sister. B. 1881. d. 1951 in Princeton, NJ. She married Paul Winterler in 1910.

Miss Helen Dukas—Albert Einstein's secretary

# APPENDIX C
## *The Rothman-Samuel family*

Here are the names of the Samuel and Rothman families that are spoken of in "Our Diary." Perhaps this will help you keep them clear in your mind!

Joseph and Emma Noé Samuel. The parents of Ruth Samuel Rothman. Emma Noé died in 1910 when Ruth was 12 years old. Then Joseph married Lina, my step-grandmother.

Regina Noé Sturmdorf—b. 1863; d. 1951. Regina was Emma Noé's half-sister. Their mother was Johanna Elbe Noé, and she was a seamstress for Sarah Bernhardt in Paris.

Children of Joseph and Emma Noé Samuel:

Hermine Samuel b. 1886 m. Jacob Levin

Florence Samuel Ravitz b. 1888

Herbert Samuel b. 1890 m. Harriet

David Samuel m. Fannie b. 1892

Milton b. 1894 m. Belle Meyerwitz (d. 1918 in flu epidemic) and Florence (Florrie) Cooper

Mabel Samuel b. 1896 m. Moe Weinberg

Ruth Samuel Rothman b. 1898 m David Arthur Rothman in 1918

Jeanette Samuel Loeb Dennis b. 1903.

# DAVID ROTHMAN's FAMILY

Parents: Chaim (Charles) Rothman and Baracha (Betty) Glick Rothman
Siblings:

Morris Rothman

a sister who died very young

Samuel Rothman who had polio and was severely crippled. He became an optometrist.

Charles "Buster" Rothman.

Children of David and Ruth Rothman:

Emma Leah Rothman (Levin) b. 1919 m. Dr. Arthur Levin on November 26, 1942; Children are Dr. Carol Levin and Dr. Diane Levin Goldstein

Arthur Ozias "Buddy" Rothman b. 1922—d. 1928

Robert Herman Rothman b. 1927. m. Audrey Ogur Rothman on November 23, 1950 Children are Charles (Chuck), Ronald (Ronnie) and Michael.

Joan Rothman Brill Kallmeyer b. 1930 m. Robert Brill on July 30, 1950; m. Paul Kallmeyer on April 1, 1976. Children are Shelley Jo Brill Kurtz b. December 9, 1951 and Leslie Lynn Davidson, b. September 26, 1953. She died on November 4, 2005 of lung cancer. Robert Brill died on January 6, 1971 of pancreatic cancer.

# *Acknowledgements*

*I would like to thank the following people for their help and faith in my ability to complete this book:*

*Bernard Kaplan, for his editing and insightful suggestions throughout the manuscript.*

*My husband, Paul R. S. Kallmeyer, for his patience and encouragement.*

*Dava Sobel, for her kind words and other help.*

*My brother, Bob Rothman and my sister, Emma Levin. Their memories were invaluable.*

*My mother, Ruth Rothman; for without her, we would have no Diary!*

*Dr. Jerold M. Lowenstein, for his permission to present his wonderful article on Albert Einstein and his theories.*

*Also: My nephew Ronald Rothman, and my daughter Shelley Jo Brill Kurtz*

*My thanks also to Michelle Wisniewski for his wonderful photo.*

*Suzanne Siegel*
*Terry O'Connor*
*Leslie Brill Davidson*
*David Arthur Rothman*

# *About the Author*

Photo by Michelle Wisniewski

JOAN BRILL is a pianist-harpsichordist who made her piano debut at Carnegie Hall following her scholarship studies at the Juilliard School. She has appeared as soloist in New York and in Florida. She was also piano soloist with the Oceanside (Long Island) Symphony, the South Fork Chamber Orchestra, the Clearwater (Florida) Symphony Orchestra, and the Tampa Bay Symphony Orchestra. Many audiences have heard her as pianist-harpsichordist with The Brill-Gaffney Trio, which has appeared all over Long Island., and with the Keys Chamber Orchestra Ensemble in Cudjoe Key, Florida.

A *Summa Cum Laude* graduate of Long Island University, she earned a Master of Music degree in piano from SUNY at Stony Brook, and then continued to polish her technique with the distinguished artist, Rosalyn Tureck. She has also studied with Josef Raieff, Leonid Hambro, Alexander Lipsky, and Martin Canin.

Joan Brill is included in The World's Who's Who of Musicians and Who's Who of American Women.

Ms. Brill is uniquely qualified to present this narration about her father's friendship with Albert Einstein, since she was present at many of the events that he describes.

978-0-595-47416-5
0-595-47416-0

CPSIA information can be obtained
at www.ICGtesting.com
Printed in the USA
BVHW031256230719
554165BV00001B/7/P

9 780595 474165